Advance praise for
Funny You Should Say That ...

"Reading each page of this book is a delight as Chuck Coburn, a highly informative guide, leads us through his personal odyssey and discovery of his psychic capabilities. In addition he is an earthy humorist and fine metaphysician who imparts extensive information about the wonders of the universe. As we identify with Chuck's experiences, we realize how we too, can access this universal bank of knowledge."

—*Marcia Emery, Ph.D.*
President, Intuitive Management Consulting Company; author

"Coburn has written a highly credible book about the discovery of psychic potentials. This is a fascinating account of an ordinary guy who has extraordinary psychic experiences. Coburn found the winning combination. He took his experiences seriously and yet humorously at the same time. Lucky for him that he had a good sense of humor to begin with!"

—*Kenneth Kelzer, M.S.W.*
Psychotherapist, author

"Chuck seems to me to be an 'old soul' who has a young way of opening doors into some quite remarkable realms, and he has a way of doing this that makes us want to be more involved. He is inviting us into his world. I believe it is the world of the future for our species. Today's paranormal and supernatural will end up being tomorrow's expanded normal and more inclusive natural."

—*Jon Klimo, Ph.D.,*
President, California Society for Psychical Studies

As beings of this earth, our life's spiritual purpose is to find out just who we are. While we are on this journey, many who are also seeking their way touch us. Through each other, we experience what we know about living.

This book is a lighthearted tale about one pilgrim who confronts his psychic nature and learns of things metaphysical while on the path of self-discovery. He shares with you his illuminating encounters with spirit guides, ghosts, shamans, healers, psychic surgeons, power spots, sacred sites, out-of-body experiences and other unexpected energy manifestations while traveling the yellow brick road to enlightenment.

A lighthearted awakening to psychic awareness

Funny You Should Say That...

A lighthearted awakening to psychic awareness

Funny You Should Say That...

Chuck Coburn

SEED CENTER
Redway • California

FUNNY YOU SHOULD SAY THAT...
Copyright © 1995 by Chuck Coburn

ISBN 0-916108-09-0

This softbound edition published by
SEED CENTER
PO Box 1700
Redway, California

First Edition
First printing 1995

96 98 99 97 95
2 4 6 8 9 7 5 3 1

LIBRARY OF CONGRESS CATALOGING-IN-PUBLICATION DATA

Coburn, Chuck, 1939–
    Funny you should say that- - : a lighthearted
awakening to psychic awareness / by Chuck
Coburn.   - - 1st ed.
        p.   cm.
    ISBN 0-916108-09-0 (perfect bound)
    1. Psychic ability.   2. Coburn, Chuck, 1939– .
3. Psychics–United States.   I. Title.
BF1031.C574   1995
133.8–dc20   95-17978
                                                    CIP

WITH SPECIAL THANKS

To the feminine energy around me,
specifically

*Gerri, my psychic guru,
who gave me my original focus;*

*Arlene, my mom,
who gave me the equipment to focus;*

*Shirl, my wife,
who helped me fine tune my focus;*

*Lori, my daughter,
who is the product of my focus;*

*And Amy, one of my spirit guides,
who focused my focus.*

Contents

Prologue

This story opens with Chapter Three.

To understand the reason this writer departed from the time-honored tradition of beginning at Chapter One, you need to know that a higher spiritual source woke me quite unexpectedly at 4:30 A.M. one cold December morning and informed me that it was time to begin my book. I was surprised at its direction, not so much at the early hour, but because I never had the slightest inclination or vaguest clue that I would become involved in such an enterprise.

Sitting at my word processor with a freshly brewed pot of coffee, I dutifully typed "Chapter One" at the top of the screen, fully anticipating that my spiritual guidance would immediately begin its dictation. I had learned sometime earlier not to question the direction of this higher source, since "it" always seemed to understand what was best for my personal growth.

I patiently sat... and waited.

Now, I am the first to agree that Chapter One would have been the logical place to begin. But, since there was a distinct absence of anything profound manifesting itself on my computer monitor after over an hour, I elected to bypass it for the moment and skip to Chapter Two.

I cleared my head and focused my efforts. Figuring that I was now well under way in the writing of this unexpected narrative, I was confident that this second chapter would unfold with much less difficulty than the previous one.

This maneuver proved equally fruitless.

For some reason for which I have no logical explanation, I modified the previously typed heading at the top of the page to read "Chapter Three." At that *very* moment, as if by magic, the words suddenly began to tumble out of some unknown location and appeared on the computer screen before me. Looking down, I observed my fingers with fascination as they moved and bumped into each other with the excitement of a new adventure, and the book began to unfold before me.

If you sense that this is going to be an unconventional story, you are correct! This will *not* be one of those stereotypical dissertations on spirituality or psychic awakening; nor, will it be similar to other esoteric how-to books that crowd the shelves of popular New Age metaphysical establishments.

Instead, you will discover that it is the tale of a common citizen, a regular guy, perhaps not unlike yourself, whose life suddenly took an unsuspecting turn at precisely 6:45 P.M. on a fall Sunday evening more than a dozen years ago! Although this book recounts the saga of one man's journey to awareness, I share it to illustrate how each of us may understand and apply the metaphysical principles that truly exist on this physical plane—once we give ourselves permission to experience them.

There are many paths out there; this story involves only one of them. However, the truth is that *all* paths ultimately lead to the same place: self-awareness, truth, growth and the understanding and acceptance of what reality truly *is.*

While reading this book, please keep in mind two basic concepts that you need to know about reality. First, reality is defined by your individual experience of it; second, *it can be changed!*

The only reason you may not have had a similar journey up to now is that you may not have been aware that it was one of your options!

How can you discover your options? Read my story!

We are *not* going to begin at the *beginning* of the story, however. Instead, we again depart from tradition and commence near the finish. (This will satisfy those who prefer to read several pages and then skip to the end to get a sense of what may lie between.)

So, I invite you to come along and explore my adventure as I experienced it. As you read the following pages, if you recognize that what you comprehend is *your* truth, then continue, observing the specific clues in your life that might lead you to *your* path as I was led to mine...

So, let's go to the end...

Which is actually the beginning...

Which begins at Chapter 3...

CHAPTER 3

The End at the Beginning

"**A**n incredibly beautiful place," I thought to myself as I surveyed the magnificent scene before me. I was perched at the top of a picturesque, 50-foot waterfall in Maui, Hawaii. For reasons I failed to fully understand, I was considering a leap off a narrow ledge into the frigid waters of the pond below.

"This has to be a power spot, a geographical energy vortex of some kind," I reasoned, trying to be rational. Yet rationality would have prevented me from even considering the action to which I was being drawn. I do not "do" heights well; nonetheless, here I was, balancing precariously close to the edge of my perch while considering a plunge into the unknown at age 50!

My wife and I were in Hawaii visiting a couple in whose house on the mainland we had been married 10 years before. They had taken us to a picturesque waterfall and pond known only to a handful of locals.

After an enjoyable swim in this secluded setting, my host, Ron, suggested I follow him up a narrow path to the top of the falls and to an outcropping of rock overlooking the pond.

Ron walked carefully to the very edge of the ledge and looked down, as if to study the water beneath. Then, drawing himself to full height, he jumped off into the pond below as he had claimed he could do.

Suddenly I was left standing alone, debating my next action. I could retrace my steps and carefully descend the path down to the pond where we had left our wives, or I could follow the more direct route taken by my friend moments before. As I stood there debating, I knew that if I were to emulate his deed it would be because I chose to do so—not because of competitive male pressure!

I couldn't believe what I was considering. My conservative nature directed me to take the safe route down; yet, I was distinctly aware of an inner feeling that was urging me to jump. All of my previous programming and my terrifying fear of heights instructed me to *not* take this course of action. Yet an exciting, inner psychic voice prompted me to take the leap...

Then again, I guess I shouldn't really have been surprised at anything I was feeling! From the moment my life began its dramatic transformation at the instant of my sudden psychic discovery some years before, nothing seemed to fit a predictable pattern. Now the *entire world* was changing. Ever since the recent observance of what the metaphysical community knew as the "Harmonic Convergence" of 1987, or even since the 1992 consciousness-awakening event known as the "11:11," the *world* had been undeniably altered. Things were different, people were different, and even the pace of living appeared to be moving much faster than before.

It was as if both Mother Earth and her inhabitants were evolving into a new form. Mankind as a whole appeared to be tuning to a higher frequency, as if undergoing evolution or transformation.

Some writers used specific phrases, such as "increased awareness," "spiritual awakening" or "elevated planetary consciousness," to characterize these phenomena. There were some who even threw out esoteric terms, such as "preparation for ascension" or "adaptation to a parallel reality." Whatever terms were used, there was no denying that something new was out there.

It was apparent on the larger worldwide scale. Major world-shaking events had occurred in a relatively short time. Just consider the few years during which Reagan's so called "Evil Empire" had collapsed, the Berlin Wall had been dismantled, and "world peace" had become a real possibility for the first time in decades, maybe centuries. We, the people of this planet, had finally begun to focus on a new set of critically important concerns: global warming, loss of the ozone layer, destruction of our rain forests and the like. We were even beginning to recycle our garbage and save our precious water in the name of conservation.

But, interestingly enough, history reveals that we could have expected these changes. Many ancient, sacred texts, including those of the Hopi, Mayan and Christian, hint about sudden and cataclysmic events affecting our planet around the end of the 20th century. These divergent spiritual dogmas each contain prophesies which foretell of events leading to this period of transformation, many of which have *already* been fulfilled.

The ancient Hopi legends, for example, inform us that our human species originally evolved when "seven sisters" arrived from the Pleiades star system, bringing with them the first seed of humankind. These ancient teachings speak of an island which sank into the water (the legendary lost continent of Atlantis, perhaps?) and of its survivors who were dispatched to the four corners of the world to become the four "colors." The red man, this prophecy suggests, was sent to the western United States to the area now known as "Four Corners"; the black man to present day Kenya, Africa; the white man to the area we call Switzerland; and the yellow man to Tibet.

One Hopi prophecy speaks of negative changes brought on when white brothers and sisters arrived as turtles, dressed in armor (Spanish conquerors dressed in medieval armor?). This prophecy was fulfilled when the red man witnessed the early stages of his culture's destruction upon the arrival of the Europeans.

Another speaks of "black ribbons" which would appear across the land (railroads and highways?). If, the legend continues, the ribbons ran north and south, all peoples of the world would come together peacefully as brothers and sisters. If they ran east and west, there would be more bad times. As we know, the white man expanded *westward* and the Hopi Nation experienced more bad times!

The Hopi prophecies specifically state that *all* must sit in the *same* circle when humankind eventually comes together, or there will be an absence of peace on earth. History validates the fact that the red man was the *only* group excluded from the League of Nations after World War I. The League soon fell apart, and World War II followed soon after that.

These prophecies speak of "cobwebs" stretching around the entire earth on which people could converse with each other (modern communication systems?), a "gourd of fire" with ashes falling from the sky (nuclear bombs?) and a "house of reflective stone on the eastern shore" where all men would meet (United Nations building on the East

Coast?). They state that men would be living in houses in the sky (astronauts in spaceships?) prior to "the final days" when humankind would experience either permanent peace or total destruction!

They say it could go either way!

The ancient Mayan culture had its prophecies too. Mayan prophecies speak of the "tides of time" rippling through the intergalactic oceans of space. They tell of a major wave of consciousness which will occur on our planet during the winter solstice of the year 2011 at the conclusion of a great cycle of 5,125 years!

These dates, as foretold by the inhabitants of the Yucatan some *25 centuries ago,* describe new positive energies never before experienced by the "density of humankind." Our Earth and its star system, according to the history of this ancient culture, will make its spiral dance into a new galactic field, allowing the Creator's awareness to have a much greater influence than ever before. Since this period will be the culmination of *many* cycles, the planet's inhabitants will begin to experience a new harmony. Humankind will "awaken" as this event draws near, providing a new understanding of who and what we really are.

The Mayans believed that the final days would be a time of *peace!*

There are some who fervently profess that the Pyramid of Giza, the world's largest and oldest man-made structure, is not merely a Pharaoh's tomb but a depository of recorded world history. They trust that one can decipher the layout of the interior passageways as if reading a calendar. This time capsule can be interpreted, they say, by using a unit of measurement known as a pyramid-inch for a year, thereby foretelling major world events from the changes in proportions found along these corridors. The documented period begins with a date over 6,000 years ago and ends shortly after the beginning of the year 2000.

Does this suggest the end of the world, or perhaps the end of the world *struggle?*

As I was standing on the brink of the cliff, staring at the water below, I recalled my recent "awakening" at the moment of the "11:11." This spiritual event, similar to the Harmonic Convergence five years prior, involved more than 144,000 souls from all parts of the planet uniting their consciousness as one. Those who actively participated focused their thoughts at the site of the Great Pyramid on January 11, 1992 (1/11/9+2=11) to help the spiritual hierarchy as they elevated the planet to a higher level of spiritual awareness.

Many elders, mystics and seers throughout the world have decreed that numerous people inhabiting physical bodies during this current period are reincarnated Atlantians. The proponents of the 11:11 believe that many souls of these past-life Atlantians had been programmed to "wake up" when they viewed these specific numbers and that their encoded instructions would direct them to join as one to raise planetary consciousness. If this awakening is necessary for our planet to evolve, who better to perform this task than the very same Atlantians who may have sank their continent and destroyed their culture many centuries before?

Some consider that even the *Bible,* the staple of Christianity, predicts the end of the world. There are fundamentalist Christian preachers smugly reminding us that many prophesied events immediately preceding the "final days" have already occurred! Yet this Christian text also mentions the 1,000 years of peace that follow.

Are these "final days" actual or symbolic? Is the world going to be physically destroyed, or will "evil" simply be eliminated and the "righteous" survive? Are the Biblical "chosen" and the New Age "spiritually aware" really the same people known by different names?

Various psychics, including Edgar Cayce and Nostradamus, perhaps the two most widely known metaphysicians who have ever lived, have discussed these cataclysmic times in great detail. Cayce, who had an extraordinary record of accuracy, spoke of major land movements leading to possible polar shifts and flooded land masses (earthquakes, volcanic eruptions?) near the end of the 20th century. Nostradamus, a well-known psychic and astrologer who lived during the 16th century, predicted numerous events hundreds of years into his future. Although his statements tend to be cryptic and difficult to understand, many claim his precision approached 90 percent. He, too, foresaw major specific changes occurring to our earth at the end of the 20th century.

Did Cayce and Nostradamus foresee the end of the world as we know it?

Diverse cultures and religions throughout the world have stories, beliefs and legends that speak of a new phase or next step in the evolution of earth. While some warn of the end of the world specifically, others suggest a new dawn. The consensus is that there will definitely be a *change!*

All these narratives predicting mass destruction can be classified as part of the negative scenario. The remaining accounts, those which suggest the world will survive with higher consciousness and karmic advancement, can be categorized as the more positive alternative.

Well, there is a strong rumor going around that the positive plan has recently been put into effect!

Thanks to the efforts of the guardian angels and enlightened souls residing on or near our planet, it now appears that the less optimistic plan will *not* unfold as previously predicted.

The spiritual hierarchy, known by many names, such as

masters, sages, gurus, avatars, ancient ones, white brother-hood and so forth, are reported to have recently confirmed that *if* the Earth remains on its present course, the collective consciousness on the planet will bring humanity to a higher or increased vibration. Groups such as the 144,000, who recently acted as one in the activation of the 11:11, may have been truly successful in raising the planetary vibrations enough to allow humankind time to get their act together.

After all, what goes around comes around, and there seems to be some new stuff going around!

This modern spiritual thought suggests that as our planet's inhabitants begin their ascension from a lower vibration of illusion and limited thought to a higher vibration, they will start to experience reality for what it *really* is.

To aid us in this process, information and wisdom which have remained sequestered in secret societies for centuries have recently been released to the public at large. For example, diverse Native American tribes and cultures have begun publicly sharing their ancient knowledge of the world. The mystery schools are taking in new students. There are those who contend that the intelligence directing unidentified flying objects (UFOs, which many cultures believe do exist) may be preparing us for these changes. There are even some who maintain that there are spiritual light beings or ancient Lemurians living underground in places, such as Mt. Shasta, California, who are now beginning to surface and share their knowledge.

Supporting this idea that we are entering a time of change are some theorists who claim that time has "speeded up." They suggest that if you could somehow transport a timepiece from the past, say 1940, and compare it with a present day clock, the current chronometer would move more quickly—additional support for Einstein's theory suggesting time is relative to the observer. Not only is present time evolving, but the measurement of what we know as time may be literally changing.

So... poised on a Hawaiian cliff, surrounded by the crashing sound of the waterfall, I was reflecting in the briefest of moments on the various life-altering changes that had brought me to this place and time.

I wondered if this were a test of some kind... A step into a new reality or higher awareness.

I was certainly not striving to prove my manhood like native boys do, who leap from the tops of high trees with a single vine or "bungi" cord tied around their ankles. I was not reacting to a dare or to pressure from a male friend. Nor was I hearing a voice from the heavens, as depicted in the Biblical story of Abraham, who was required to test his faith with the life of his young son.

Instead, I sensed on a deep inner level that I was about to let go of old ways that I needed to discard. I was about to open a new door, cross a threshold and change my reality. Fairly certain now that I was going to jump, I had to trust that there was a new threshold to cross and that I was about to cross it.

The next thing I knew, I had stepped out into the air...

CHAPTER 4

The Beginning

To fully understand what followed that leap, I must return to the beginning of my tale. The process, the path of *getting* to that moment at the waterfall, is a significant aspect. The path *is* the journey; to understand the journey, one must understand the path...

ONCE UPON A TIME...

(Because this portion of my tale begins with "Once upon a time," this doesn't mean it's not a true story; it is. Although most books that begin in this fashion are fictional, they are written for the express purpose of illustrating lessons and revealing hidden meanings contained therein, and this book most definitely meets those criteria.)

Once upon a time I was born... and my experience of my universe began.

My earliest remembered formal training in this new earth-environment occurred during my formative pre-school years. During this time I acquired many of life's useful skills, such as stacking blocks—early construction techniques that were to serve me well in my chosen profession in later years, and hide-and-seek—dealing with peer group, win-at-all-cost competitiveness.

As my reality-preparedness education advanced, I moved on to grammar school, where I earned some highly notable achievements. These included being appointed blackboard monitor *for two weeks in a row*, being the first in my class to memorize my seven-times multiplication tables and, on a dare, kissing a real cutie named Ann without getting punched!

In seventh grade, I even achieved the near impossible—going steady for *32 days straight* without my parents finding out!

Anyway... having mastered all the mandatory requirements and skills necessary at this level, I entered high school. There I did all the very insecure things one does during that time of one's life; then I ventured off to college, got married and began my grown-up life!

By the time I reached age 35, I was cruising through life with the statistically average family: a wife, a son, a daughter, a dog, two cats, a mortgage and the appropriate number of credit card payments. I had become a very successful general contractor in a third-generation family business, and I resided comfortably in a quiet suburban community in the San Francisco Bay Area.

I suppose my principal goal in life was to acquire the same middle class values and accomplishments that my parents had effectively obtained. I was living a very predictable and structured life, following all the familiar, conservative patterns taught to me since childhood. Although I was struggling in a soon-to-end marriage that neither of us seemed to fully understand, it was my belief that I was happy. Why shouldn't I be? I had it all: a successful business, a wonderful family, the good life!

And then one day my life took an *abrupt* change of course, leading me to unexpectedly discover my inherent psychic nature.

(Ever notice that most stories beginning with "Once upon a time... " subsequently begin a paragraph with "And then one day... "? This generally serves to alert us that we are about to encounter a major change in the story line—here comes the portion of the story which leads to the lessons we can learn—and who am I to break tradition?)

It was at this time, in my seemingly secure existence, that I met my next door neighbor's sister while attending a social gathering at his house. During casual cocktail party conversation, she shared an experience of a recent weekend seminar, enthusiastically claiming that it had radically changed her life. By the end of the evening she had persuaded me to attend a repeat presentation of this workshop. She convinced me that it would be as positive an experience as the seminar's name "YES" suggests.

I was definitely not a seminar junkie, yet I was drawn to her enthusiasm for what she had undergone. She told me that her life experience, like mine, had been quite happy and contented, but that she had sensed something "missing" and had found "it" at this weekend retreat.

She was right. The seminar was *dynamite!* From the very moment it began, I was absolutely absorbed in an encounter with brand new ideas—new to me at least.

The program began with an activity that required us to introduce and describe ourselves to a stranger sitting nearby. Then, unexpectedly, we were required to report on what we *heard* to the rest of the class. In this very first experience we realized that we were so involved in *ourselves* that few of us had paid attention to what our partner had said. This exercise was designed to illustrate the limitations of our individual awareness in our day-to-day lives. Jan and Hardy, our seminar leaders, guaranteed to change all that by the time the seminar was over!

As the weekend progressed, many experiences we collectively encountered encouraged us to touch and express long-repressed emotions, such as fear, joy, anger and sadness. I came to realize that expressing sadness was *very* difficult for me, yet I found that others could do this quite easily. Although anger seems somewhat easier for men to verbalize, I was truly amazed that many of my classmates had almost totally blocked the verbalization of this emotion for most of their lives.

It became readily apparent to all of us by the end of the first day that while this retreat was about many things, it was primarily designed to encourage us to experience our feelings and our emotions... on the way to the discovery of our inner selves. We soon realized that the deeper we got in touch with these sensations, the more we became truly aware of ourselves and who we really were. But it wasn't until this weekend was ending that I discovered just how wide the door to this awareness had opened!

The weekend continued. At the beginning of the third and final day we were informed that it was time for us to demonstrate some of the self-awareness we had learned during the previous two days. In a morning exercise we each placed our driver's license into a separate envelope and sealed it. After the envelopes were shuffled, we randomly selected one of the envelopes from the pile and were asked to sense or intuit whose envelope we had drawn, *without opening it!* At the conclusion of the exercise, I reviewed the physical features shown on the license. I was shocked to find that, from the group of 30, I had *accurately identified* the individual whose photo peered out when I opened my sealed envelope!

Equally astonishing, a statistically high percentage of my classmates had similarly successful experiences. Furthermore, many of those who did not correctly identify the specific individual discovered that they had accurately predicted many physical characteristics of the person whose license was in the envelope they held.

During this final day we were to experience additional intuitive hits by tuning in to our newly discovered awareness. But the last event of the seminar was *the* clincher!

We were ushered into a room where several dozen strangers were seated, each having an empty chair in front of him or her. Hardy introduced them as clairvoyants, accomplished in the art of thought transference. After each of us was paired with a psychic, we were provided with just the name, age and location of a known acquaintance of our partner. We were then instructed to describe this acquaintance in specific detail. The psychics seated in front of us held a "thought picture" of the subject while we composed our stories. When the exercise was finished, our partners handed us written descriptions and photographs of our "targets" from sealed containers resting beneath their chairs.

I was dead right... again!

My target was a retired Montana cowboy, whom I described in great detail. I had correctly identified him by appearance, profession, personal hobbies, the number and sex of his children and several of his personal traits. As evident from the image that stared back at me from a color photograph, I had been accurate even to the color of his red and white suspenders, favorites he wore when he went fishing.

We were *then* informed that we were not working with professional psychics at all, but with previous graduates from this seminar. They were normal, regular people, just like ourselves, who had recently completed the same workshop a few months before.

Wasn't it interesting, we were asked, how perceptive we became once we were convinced that we were working with telepathic psychics possessing unique and specially trained abilities? We were *all* psychically aware or perceptive once we gave ourselves permission to tune into the natural ability we each have built into our originally issued physical equipment.

As the seminar came to its conclusion, Hardy and Jan reminded us that this weekend experience had provided us with both opportunity and permission to experience our emotions to a much greater degree than ever previously imagined. We learned it was now O.K. to cry (tough one for me, raised with the notion that men *do not* cry); it was now O.K. to be angry (an emotion many believed led to trouble and should be suppressed). We were reminded that as we used this oft-neglected tool, doors to our natural intuition would open as never before.

Most of us, beginning in early childhood, had learned to deny the full experience of our own emotions. As a result, to one degree or another we had all missed much of what life had been originally designed to offer.

We now had a new way of being!

And it felt good!

CHAPTER 5

First Experience

As the workshop closed, we all exchanged the customary hugs and promises to stay in contact with each other. About a dozen of us agreed to have dinner together in order to compare experiences and to continue celebrating our increased sense of personal awareness.

A local member of our group recommended a nearby, quiet restaurant to which we exuberantly headed. We jockeyed for specific places at the table, and I found myself seated next to a middle-aged, pleasant-looking woman named Susan. It was her license which I had correctly identified during the eye-opening experience earlier that morning.

We all had a wonderful time, eagerly sharing our newly discovered emotions with people to whom we had grown quite attached during these precious few days. We exchanged addresses, though we knew that we would probably never get together again in spite of all our good intentions.

As we were enjoying our after-dinner coffee, Susan casually mentioned in an innocent, matter-of-fact voice that she was intrigued by my success with several of the intuitive processes during the seminar. She continued by listing some specifics I had correctly identified before opening the sealed envelope containing her driver's license.

I responded that I, too, had been amazed at my success. I speculated, however, that I would most likely fail should I ever attempt to repeat the exercise in the future.

Susan promptly rejoined that she wasn't surprised at all. Leaning toward me as if to share a confidence, she whispered that she *knew* from the moment we met that I possessed an extrasensory gift. She stated emphatically that it was *not* just a coincidence that we had ended up being partners and that her observations regarding my success had merely confirmed her previous knowing!

Addressing what must have been a puzzled look on my face, she revealed that *she* was a professional *psychic*, having flown up from southern California to attend the workshop because of her friendship with Hardy and Jan. She went on to say that it was important I understand that I was *very* psychic. Furthermore, she was certain that a major part of my life's purpose was to use this natural ability for the benefit of *others*!

Now, you have to know that I wasn't even sure what a psychic was, and I doubted that she could be one, since she looked quite normal. After all, the old movies generally portrayed psychics as short, wearing ill-matched, second-hand clothing and looking like they had just escaped from a carnival!

Then, quite unexpectedly, Susan turned her gaze to the ceiling as if to reply to a question posed from above her head and over her shoulder. Following the direction of her gaze, yet seeing nothing, I debated about asking what had suddenly drawn her attention, but I decided to remain silent.

"My spirit guides," she said, anticipating my question while maintaining her stare at a point in the air above the table. Holding up her hand to suspend further questions, she completed her silent exchange with whatever she seemed to perceive was up there.

"Spirit guides?" I asked quietly when she turned back to me, wondering whether I really wanted to pursue this whole line of thought with someone who had apparently gone over the edge. At the same time, I was fascinated and extremely curious about the bizarre situation.

She briefly explained that guides were her spiritual helpers, much like angels. They talked to her and gave her guidance.

"Of course," I replied in a low tone. I was wondering just how I could politely extricate myself from this bizarre dialogue. She returned her gaze to the ceiling again as if to complete a thought.

After a few moments of a scene that was clearly out of "Pretend Corner," down the block beyond *Mr. Roger's Neighborhood*, she abruptly concluded her private conversation. Turning back to me, she asked if I would be willing to try something which would *prove* that I truly had a psychic gift.

Having no other place to go and definitely intrigued, I said something like, "Sure, why not?" At the same time I felt apprehensive about what might occur.

Straightening up, she issued clear and specific instructions for me to target an individual within view of where we sat. She informed me that her guides would help me in detecting specific information about the person I had chosen and would provide me the convincing proof that I required.

"Be sure it's someone you have never met," she cautioned.

I peered out from the raised platform overlooking the

lower floor of our pleasantly decorated Italian restaurant. Arbitrarily, I selected a fairly attractive woman about 30, wearing a fashionably tailored red dress, seated in a booth approximately 20 feet from where we sat.

Acknowledging my choice, Susan directed me to close my eyes and give myself complete permission to visualize a future event concerning the woman I had designated. She again assured me that her spirit helpers would assist me and that I should just let it happen.

If she meant to calm me with the assurance that her mysterious voices were going to speak to *me*, she had not read the situation accurately! Nevertheless, she was so convincing in her enthusiasm for whatever she thought might happen that I found myself caught up in this entire procedure in spite of the consequences.

"Make up a story as you did with my driver's license, and my guides will take care of the details," she advised.

With my heart making thumping noises that I thought might alert others at the table, I closed my eyes, certain that everyone in the restaurant would be staring directly at me. Susan coached me, advising me to breathe slowly and not to rush. She continued to remind me that I would receive whatever information her guides wanted me to know.

Obeying, I closed my eyes and waited for something to happen.

Nothing did!

"Don't try so hard," she cautioned. "You're doing fine; just let it happen."

Slowly, after a brief time elapsed, I became aware of what I can best describe as a visualization beginning to emerge in my mind's eye. The experience was not unlike playing a child's game in which a heroine is left in a perilous situation by a storyteller, and you use your imagination to construct an immediate means of rescuing her with some degree of plausibility.

Susan repeated the instruction to "just let it happen" several more times. I cautiously began to fantasize that my heroine, the lady in the red dress, was engaged in what seemed to be a fight or struggle. I could see a man's hands grasping at her throat as if attempting to strangle her. After a brief struggle she fell to the floor, the hands remaining tightly wrapped around her neck.

As my imagined mental picture expanded, I became aware of another individual, a very large and clearly overweight person dressed in what I assumed was a white mechanic's uniform with a bright green belt at the waist. This third person seemed to be sitting on the woman, punching her repeatedly in the chest and upper body.

Then it was over! Only, unlike the children's game, I had not saved her from the hands of the villains!

I opened my eyes and, after some coaxing, related the story to Susan as I had experienced it. She listened quietly as I unraveled the wildly imaginative yarn. I felt completely drained, as if I had physically taken part in the struggle I had just created in my imaginative mind to amuse my unusual dinner companion.

After a pause that seemed hours long, I asked her what was next. A logical query, I thought, after following her strange instructions and rules.

"I guess you'll just have to wait and see," she responded.

I glanced over to the dinner table where my target was peacefully enjoying her meal. Everything seemed very much in order, nothing the least bit threatening in the offing.

As I was kicking around the odds of this elaborate fight scene actually taking place in this quiet and peaceful restaurant, I heard my name called from the other end of the table. In an attempt to dismiss what I had just envisioned, I shifted my attention to the conversation I was invited to enter.

About 15 minutes later, as we were engrossed in the laboriously detailed process of dividing the dinner check to second decimal accuracy, we were suddenly startled by a loud shout emanating from a nearby table.

My lady in the red dress had suddenly bolted to her feet and appeared to be choking, unable to breathe!

Her male companion, responding to her desperate situation, reached over and placed his hands *around her neck* in what was most likely an instinctive reaction to her inability to breathe. Struggling, she dropped to the floor, his hands still clutched tightly around her throat. Just then, a patron from a distant table rushed over, loudly declaring that she had training in CPR. This third person immediately straddled the struggling body on the floor and began *pounding on her chest* to dislodge whatever was stuck in her windpipe!

It was just as I had foreseen, except instead of *being* choked, she was *choking* on some food!

The difference between what I had visualized and what actually took place was due to misinterpretation. The "fight" I'd seen was in reality an offer of assistance. Instead of my pretty lady being strangled, the hands at her throat were trying to help. Rather than someone pounding her chest in a fight, someone was actually attempting to save her life!

As I replayed what I had recently seen in my mind, I realized that the rescuer *was* just as I had described her. What I assumed to be a mechanic's uniform was, however, a white pantsuit.

I know the first words out of my mouth were similar to the censored expletives that football coaches often shout just before the TV cameras cut away from the closeup shots on Monday Night Football. I don't know if I was more concerned about the spilt coffee stains on my shirt or the soiled underwear I was certain I now wore.

Funny You Should Say That...

By now, the choking lady had begun to recover, and it appeared she would be O.K.... but my own future wasn't so certain!

Did what I just saw really happen?

... And if it did, was I the cause of it?

... And if so, was I in league with the devil?

Needless to say, I was in for a long, sleepless night!

CHAPTER 6

All Alone

I returned home that evening after having experienced more than a lifetime of events in just three short days. To say that I was on an emotional high would be the understatement of the year! I reviewed all that had happened over and over in my mind, not really believing what I knew had occurred.

I wandered aimlessly around the house. Eventually I found myself in the back yard reflecting on the entire weekend, seated in one of those old, uncomfortable, metal patio chairs that always find their way into back yards. I felt wonderfully alive, having rediscovered the use of my seldom-expressed emotions. Like a kid with a new toy I felt excited, but fearful of testing its limits and determining just what it could do.

My mind repeatedly returned to the episode at dinner where I had accurately predetermined an event, and a *dramatic* event at that, several minutes *before* it occurred. What had happened must have been a fantasy, I thought; it couldn't actually have taken place. It was not unlike the entertaining tales that appeared in science fiction comic books I'd read as a child. But I knew those stories never really happened, not really. Decades ago I had reluctantly accepted the fact that I did not have supernatural powers. I learned, for example, I could never be like Superman, in spite of many childhood, body-bruising attempts to learn how to fly. (That X-ray vision thing, though, might have offered some good insights.)

Life had taught me that reality was what you could *see* or *feel* and that anything else was fantasy or wishful thinking. Real was real, and that was that! This notion had been reinforced repeatedly, such as when my boyhood friend Harry and I sent away for one of those throw-your-voice devices advertised for $19.95 in the back of *Boy's Life*. As we grew up, we discovered those things never actually worked.

There was the time Harry and I bought a book on mental telepathy. We had been told by Harry's older brother that by staring at the back of someone's neck while thinking the phrase "turn around," you could easily maneuver and control others. Although Harry seemed to have some success, I concluded that it was because he would "break wind" while standing fairly close to his target, unfairly skewing his claimed metaphysical results.

So here I was, sitting in the back yard, freezing my assorted appendages at 10:00 P.M. on an October Sunday night while attempting to redefine reality from my new perspective. I had clearly experienced one of those life-altering events reported in books on famous people. But, hey, I was no one special, just an ordinary guy who thought he had a fair understanding of life even though he had never been issued an operating manual.

I began to speculate that if this paranormal experience

could occur within the controlled environment of the workshop, and again when guided by Susan at dinner, then maybe I could switch it on by myself.

On the other hand, what if it began to happen spontaneously and I couldn't control it? I began to consider whether I really wanted the responsibility of knowing what was going to happen before it occurred. What if I knew someone was going to die or something? The thought could be downright scary.

What I had recently experienced was definitely unusual or abnormal by almost anyone's measurement, and I wasn't sure I wanted to be different. After all, how many years did it take to get things the way I thought I wanted them? I fit into my circle of friends just fine, thank you, and I was not convinced that I wanted my life to change. Furthermore, TV's Mr. Rogers had repeatedly told me that he liked me just the way I was!

At the same time, whatever was happening to me was intriguing... no, it was *fascinating*, and I knew there was no way I was going to be able to leave this thing alone!

As I looked out on the late night darkness, I began to contemplate how I might induce another psychic experience. Again concern arose: what if I did and it turned out to be another negative occurrence, *might I be the cause of it?* What if I set something in motion over which I had no control? What if this thing got out of hand?

Nonetheless, I took a deep breath... closed my eyes... and waited for a thought-picture to begin forming as before.

Nothing happened.

I waited for a considerable time, and nothing kept happening. This special, increased awareness simply told me that it was cold and that I was extremely tired from all that had come my way since Friday morning. I decided to abandon this outpost on the edge of weirdness and go inside to bed.

As I ambled through the house turning off lights, for absolutely no apparent reason I began to think about playing tennis. I thought it odd since I had no particular interest in the sport. The more this idle thought occupied my mind, however, the more I noticed that the court surface I mentally pictured was painted an odd green color.

Sitting on the edge of the bed, unloosening my shoes, I realized that there was only one pair of feet on this court. Unusual, I thought; it was my understanding that it took at least two players to make the game work. I concluded they were female feet because the socks had those cute, fuzzy little balls dangling from the back. The feet, one of which was wrapped in something like a support bandage, seemed to float up from the court and drift off to my left.

Though I attempted to dismiss the thought, the picture kept reappearing in my mind—an odd colored court and a pair of feet with one apparently injured, floating up, up and away...

I wasn't "seeing" it like I see a book or painting. It was more like a nagging thought or idea lingering in the back of my mind while I tried to focus on something else. This thought was locked in now, repeating over and over on the projection screen in my head like a stuck loop of film.

As I turned off the last light and snuggled into my bed, the scene continued to replay. After reviewing the reruns repeatedly, I gave up trying to sleep, slipped on my bathrobe and returned to the back yard where my preoccupation originated. Nothing much had changed since I had left, other than it had gotten colder.

Then I got it!

The court that I had been visualizing actually existed in a nearby neighbor's yard! Although it was usually only observable from my vantage point in the daylight, it could be seen at this time of year when the leaves began dropping from the trees.

I peered in the direction of the court to verify the odd surface color in the dark. It occurred to me that Judy, the woman whose court I was seeing, would most likely wear the cutesy tennis socks I'd seen in my "vision."

In a flash I was in my house, searching for her phone number in our neighborhood pool club directory, remembering that she was also a member. If it were her feet, perhaps she could give me confirmation about the bandage. It was late, but I could not wait until morning. From my position I could just make out a light on in her front room, so I assumed she was still up and about.

I realized that I would have to provide some plausible explanation for my unusual call because I would risk losing my credibility in our social circle if I were wrong. It's not often that one makes a telephone call late on a Sunday night to confirm a full-on vision! Vision—wasn't that what the guys in the *Old Testament* used to have? But I phoned her anyway, apologized for the lateness of my call, and gave her a condensed version of what I had experienced.

After what had to be a millennium of silence, she began to chuckle in the wonderful way one does when something is suddenly understood. Without even questioning the highly unusual nature of my late call, she laughed a second time.

"You know… " She paused.

"FUNNY YOU SHOULD SAY THAT… !"

She went on to describe the events of *her* weekend, relating in great detail how she had *sprained her ankle* the day before… *playing tennis* on her court! *And,* if that were not enough, she added that she and her husband had just concluded the purchase of a new house. They would be *moving* as soon as they could sell their home!

My mind could hardly accept what I had just heard!

Her ankle had been sprained (the bandage) and they were going to move from their house (feet leaving the tennis court)! Furthermore, the new home was located in the same direction—as seen from my back yard—as the feet had drifted in my psychic visualization.

It had happened again!

Hanging up the telephone, I decided I was *not* about to go outside again; if I did, I just might encounter one of those scary things that as a kid I knew hid in the shadows...

And I didn't think I could deal with that just then!

CHAPTER 7

Why Me?

T he validation of this second psychic experience left me more confused than ever. The vision of the feet, one ankle bandaged, floating off the odd-colored tennis court had definitely been authenticated by both the sprain and the house for sale!

I began to desperately search for the commonality between the two events. I realized that my first psychic knowing, the choking scene in the restaurant, involved a situation which had not yet occurred. I somehow knew that the woman in the red dress was going to choke *before* it happened. Yet my second paranormal experience, the tennis court scene, was quite different; I knew on some psychic level what had occurred well *after* the incident. Were these simply two isolated incidents? Would such episodes recur? Although I was confused and apprehensive, there was an inner desire for another psychic experience.

It wasn't until years later that I realized how my reaction to these initial paranormal experiences had set the course for my continued psychic opening. I would learn that two requisites are necessary if one is to continue to develop the natural psychic abilities each of us inherently possesses.

The first requirement is *acknowledgment*—acknowledging that a paranormal experience actually transpired and could not be casually dismissed with a rational explanation. The second is *acceptance*—accepting not only that these unprecedented experiences happened, but also accepting that they could be the precursors of future encounters with the unexplainable. Not an easy assignment, given the natural fear that I somehow had activated a mysterious, inner power or force that I could neither understand nor control.

As you might expect, I had become somewhat paranoid, almost expecting to hear strange voices or the weird music indicating that I was entering "The Twilight Zone."

Yet I was pragmatic and could generally count on my rationality and logic in new situations. Even as a kid I often accurately anticipated the ending prior to the last reel of the Western movies I faithfully followed. I invariably solved the murder mystery before the last chapter of the *Hardy Boys*, the adventure books I read in grammar school. Most likely I would have been ahead of Nancy Drew as well, except that she was a girl, and boys wouldn't be caught dead reading *Nancy Drew*.

Now, Freddy the Pig would have known what to do—he was the best of the bunch!

For those of you whose education is incomplete and who have never met Freddy the Pig, Freddy was the hero in a series of books I remember reading in my early, learning-to-read years, immediately following the adventures of Dick and Jane and their beloved dog Spot. Freddy was cool; he casually stumbled through life much like Peter Falk in the

"Colombo" series on television. He always seemed to have the solution well in hand; he was always in control. There is an old saying, "Never mess with pigs... you'll just get dirty and *they* love it."

But sometimes, one is too close to a situation to really understand what has occurred. It took me some time to fully comprehend that my workshop experience, one of the most *profound, emotionally-freeing, self-validating* three days of my life, must have contributed to my transformation and newly found personal power. The weekend had been about many things, including feeling, knowing and trusting. It was also about being positive, being accountable for my own emotions and *not* being responsible for or reacting to the feelings of others.

The seminar had provided an opportunity for me to let go of doubt and fear. These negative and nonproductive emotions not only limit our capacity to create positively, but arouse anxiety and increase our fear. I was slowly beginning to comprehend that by releasing my emotional blockage, I had triggered the experience.

Yet for every question answered and concept understood, there were additional concerns to take their place—questions that began with "what," "why" and "how." *What* was I supposed to do with this newly found ability; *why* was this suddenly happening to me; *how* was I to use this "gift"?

Moreover, were there other "powers" in this package? (Maybe flying like Superman wasn't totally out of the question after all!) What would it be like if I knew what people around me were thinking or what would happen before others did? My mind raced with possibilities. If I could successfully harness this power, I could predict which horse would win the Derby or which way the dice would fall before they were thrown.

After reviewing endless scenarios, I decided to try to

predict a specific event that might take place in the immediate future, one that could be easily validated visually. I began by previewing the upcoming day, settling on the morning commute to work. That ought to be a good test, I thought, since one encounters almost anything during a typical Monday morning rush hour.

So, while lying in bed, with sleep being one of my last options, my mind began to trace the route I unfailingly drove each workday morning. I visualized myself pulling out of the garage and beginning the drive to the downtown area that leads to a freeway on-ramp.

While mentally reviewing the journey I knew like the back of my hand, I realized that I was exhausted. Sleep began to make its demands on my tired body. As I let go of my thoughts, it occurred to me that I was focusing on a particular intersection in a quiet neighborhood. It was as if I were replaying a movie that had frozen on one specific frame.

Then, without warning, the still picture shifted into motion. I saw a yellow car swerve and collide with a water hydrant. The scene continued to unfold, and I could see kids playing in the water as it gushed from the broken pipe. The image then took on a cartoon-like quality as the street turned into a river and houses started drifting down the street like they were riding on a magic carpet...

I awoke to the sound of the early morning alarm clock and instantly recalled the street scene visualized as I was falling asleep. I wondered if it were all a dream, not really sure when sleep affected the process. I repeatedly reviewed what I could remember, reflecting on the dream-like quality of the experience.

As I walked out of the house, I felt apprehensive about driving by *the* intersection. Logic and reason suggested that the fantasy scenario could have been a recollection of an old Bowery Boys movie I had recently seen on late night TV. Perhaps I had simply envisioned one of those corny old 1940's movies.

Anxiety and nervousness formed a partnership in my stomach as I began the drive downtown. If it had been a dream, I wondered what the symbols of the car and water represented. I knew enough about dreams to know their images generally contain hidden meanings.

About a block from the intersection in question, I eased my car to the curb and stopped. I wanted to light a cigarette, as if I were dramatically involved in an old Bogart movie—I almost forgot that I had quit smoking years before. Feeling ridiculous, I pulled back into the flow of traffic and drove that final, extremely long block to *the* intersection. Driving past it, I turned my head and looked down the street.

Nothing!!!

Nothing but the normal stuff of which quiet, middle-class neighborhoods are made. There was no yellow car, no water in the street, nothing unusual or out of the norm. Incredibly disappointed yet greatly relieved, I continued driving to work.

Tuesday morning I again approached that particular neighborhood street crossing with caution, and as I passed, I saw that it looked quite similar to the previous morning, or to any other morning for that matter.

Wednesday morning, having put the precognitive event out of my mind, I was driving through town toward the freeway when I casually glanced down the side street on which I had been focusing the past two days.

I could hardly believe my eyes: A yellow car with its front end wrapped around a hydrant... a gusher shooting 20 feet in the air... and water *everywhere!*

What I had seen Sunday night occurred Wednesday morning!

Had this precognitive experience been a dream or a conscious psychic vision? It is sometimes difficult to differentiate between the two since, in a broad sense, they are both psychic experiences. What is more important is to recognize the parallel elements in each of these paranormal occurrences.

All the psychic events that took place after the seminar—the restaurant occurrence, the tennis court visualization, and now the precognitive event with the fire hydrant—had several features in common. Each had been solicited, each centered on a dramatic event involving an accident or injury, and each concerned people or situations on the periphery of my life. The fact that the choking, the ankle injury and the auto accident had all been negative events was most unnerving.

Why was I being forewarned? Was I supposed to have interceded and prevented these occurrences from taking place? Would there be more?

Research parapsychologists would likely agree that one's initial psychic experiences often occur around negative events. Why? Negative situations are often threatening or act as a warning and, therefore, are more noticeable. As an example, a nightmare is the dream most often remembered because it deals primarily with a fear or negative images. Nightmares are often simply dreams that are dramatized in an attempt to get our attention. We pay more attention to negative news—just tune in to the evening broadcast or examine the headlines of a local newspaper if you have doubts.

In my particular case, the choking lady in the red dress certainly caught my attention. Had I been presented a more positive event, it might have gone unnoticed or been dismissed as a hunch or lucky guess.

Survival and well-being are basic human instincts, and fear is an emotion that often triggers, or results from, the natural functioning of our inbred psychic intuition. Though fear is usually perceived as a negative feeling, a psychic warning is more likely to accompany a fearful situation than a positive one. Primitive people knew this and perceived fear as their natural ally. In our modern society, unfortunately, we often ignore this psychic input in our haste to avoid fearful situations.

An unnoticed psychic perception has little value. As religion requires faith of the heart, psychic intuition requires acceptance and belief. Both provide well-being and comfort if we are willing to open to their messages.

So… why did the fire hydrant event take three days to occur? Because, although I had accurately precognized this event, *I forgot to specify the time frame!*

CHAPTER 8

Learning a Major Lesson

In the weeks following my experience with the fire hydrant, I paid constant attention to each thought, daydream, or idle mind chatter that came to, and through, my awareness. Although introduced to a new source of knowledge with an unknown purpose, I was beginning to enjoy the distinctive feelings which accompanied it.

I was discovering an unknown part of myself, and I was eager to explore it, except, of course, its dark and scary corners. The little kid in me viewed all of this as if I had suddenly and inexplicably been caught up in a dream, or as if I were an actor in a movie playing a part.

At the same time, it was disconcerting to be "different." How many years had I conformed, doing what was necessary to be like everyone else—joining the correct college fraternity, dressing in the accepted style, blending in?

Several weeks passed and, other than basking in the glow of my newly discovered emotions, nothing of a psychic nature occurred. Then, as "coincidence" would have it, business required that I be in Reno, Nevada.

Reno is the "Greatest Little City in the World," or so we're informed by the motto emblazoned on local brochures and cocktail napkins. One of Reno's main attractions involves green, felt-covered tables where people wager on the number of dots showing uppermost at the eventual stationary position of two small, six sided, dot covered cubes thrown by one of the participants—a.k.a. craps tables!

The idea had *not* been entirely lost to me that if I used my psychic ability to determine the eventual outcome of a pair of dice *before* they were rolled, my chances of winning could be greatly enhanced. I decided to put my newfound talent to good use, while also having a little fun at the tables.

As I entered the main lobby of one of the casinos, I was aware of the drama of the moment. If this *were* a movie, Robert Redford would enter and look slowly around the room. After narrowing his eyes and setting his jaw, he would saunter to a table and stand next to a gorgeous woman wearing a low-cut, sequined dress.

I couldn't find the gorgeous woman!

I wandered over to a nearby table and wedged myself into a group of players who seemed to be winning, judging by the rows of chips displayed in racks in front of them. As I became absorbed in the action at the table, I had a "feeling" I was about to receive instructions of a psychic nature.

I waited.

"Don't bet until you have the dice," suddenly whispered a firm voice inside my head. I turned around to assure myself that the voice did not originate from a nearby player... or the gorgeous woman.

"Not yet," it seemed to caution.

The dice had been held for an extended period by several players who, along with almost everyone else except the casino management, were winning a great deal of money on the majority of rolls of the dice.

Now, if you have ever been at a craps table, you know that *you* are in control when *you* throw the dice. It is an extremely exciting moment if you do well because not only are you winning money, but everyone who is betting with you is also winning and shouting encouragement; you become a local folk hero.

"Wait until it is your turn," nagged the inner thought.

Eventually the dice were placed in front of me. It was my turn.

I placed a sizable wager on the line, picked up the dice and immediately rolled a 12.

"Craps, you lose," said the stick man to a chorus of groans. The odds are more than 30 to 1 against that happening, and, ironically, it's the most unlikely way in which to lose!

"Maybe I wasn't ready; maybe I didn't hold them right," I muttered to myself, placing a new wager, larger than the first.

I tossed the dice again, this time establishing a point of eight. All I had to do was make another eight before I rolled a seven and I would win. It was a good number because there are many combinations of ways to throw an eight.

Listening quietly, I heard the inner voice in my head say, *"You* are in control!"

So I took the odds, thereby increasing my bet to the maximum amount allowed. I placed bets on *all* the numbers other than seven, the only number of the 11 possible which could cause me to lose all my bets. If I could roll any number *other* than a seven, I would win.

I rolled a *seven!!!*

To make a very long and *painful* story short, I played

for awhile, attempting to isolate the same special knowing which had previously guided and informed me so successfully. I was apparently experiencing some severe technical difficulties with the audio portion of my programming because every bet I wagered I lost!

I decided to relocate to the roulette table and bet on red or black, basically 50/50 odds and much less confusing.

I bet on a color and promptly lost. I bet again. I lost again. Then I bet opposite what I thought was going to happen. I lost. I then bet opposite what I thought was going to happen, but before the ball stopped bouncing around the wheel to land on a color, I changed my bet to the opposite of that, and I *still* lost.

Ten times I bet; *ten times I lost!*

I remembered reading that the odds of winning *or* losing 10 times in a row are many millions to one. Was some higher source trying to tell me something? Were there lessons here?

The answer to both questions was a resounding YES! I had been presented with two concepts that took me some time to understand fully.

First, the gift I had been given was precious and was not to be misused.

As stated in Manly Hall's *The Secret Teachings of All Ages,* "The most dangerous form of black magic is the scientific perversion of occult power for the *gratification of personal desire* (italics mine). Its less complex and more universal form is human selfishness, for selfishness is the fundamental cause of worldly evil."

We can trace the modern use of "black magic" back to the Hermes mystery schools, where it was taught that "What the mind can conceive and believe, the mind can achieve."

But Hermes did not write it as a glorification of the mind; he wrote it as a *warning*—a warning not to misuse it!

This gift of mine was to be used explicitly for good and rightful purposes, *not* for material gain, or more specifically, non-spiritual enterprises. I would later understand the specific purpose for my gift and also learn how to implement metaphysical principles for creating what I need— not for my comfort, but for my education and growth. This lesson had to be *experienced,* the most effective means of learning.

The second concept I was being taught was that there is no such thing as "coincidence." Virtually everything one does, everything that occurs, is for a purpose. Further, occurrences are created specifically *by the person experiencing them.* So, instead of believing that one's major learning events simply arise because of randomness or coincidence, consider that there is most often an explicit reason for their occurrence.

You have, no doubt, heard the expression, "We create our own reality." It's true. The reality we create is for our experience of it. We are the creators of our own little mini-universes, and we play by the rules, or belief systems, we have created.

The concept of "synchronicity," which is similar to the notion of "coincidence," suggests that we each create the significant events we experience for specific purposes. In addition, this process is often a vehicle used by our higher, spiritual self to present us with opportunities for learning lessons—the reason we are in physical form.

I have a sweatshirt, which I often wear, that states this principle in another way: "COINCIDENCE, GOD'S WAY OF REMAINING ANONYMOUS!"

Following this expensive field trip to Reno, I saw that there were some valuable lessons I needed to assimilate. I began to realize that I required specific direction if I were to understand and properly use this wonderful gift. I had to learn to master its use and channel it properly. I needed to find someone who could help me understand what was happening, as well as what to do with it. Susan, the mysterious woman from the seminar, lived somewhere in Los Angeles, but I didn't know how to contact her, and I didn't know anyone else versed in this matter.

I *had* learned a few things, though. I learned *not* to waste or misuse this ability. I also learned that changing my profession to that of a professional gambler was slightly premature.

Several weeks went by, and there were few people with whom I could confide who would not conclude I had gone "loony tunes." I was certainly *not* going to mention these experiences to friends in casual, cocktail-party conversation. I could just imagine their reaction to the disclosure that my life had completely changed because I was having psychic revelations! I probably would have received snide comments ranging from "Excuse me, you had a what?" to "O.K., so tell me what I'm thinking right now!" So I kept the secret to myself.

However, I did share some of my experiences with several women who worked in a restaurant where I ate lunch almost daily. Recounting the episodes where I had "known things," I offered to "read" for several of them in exchange for their feedback. Initially there were funny looks and stifled laughter, but one waitress said she would be open to such an experience. A few days later, after the lunch hour rush, the two of us settled into a quiet booth where we wouldn't be interrupted. I took several deep breath, closed my eyes, and waited...

Funny You Should Say That...

I waited some more...
Nothing... not even static.
Then, mercifully, someone called her name, and I found a way to slip out, mumbling that maybe I'd get back to her... much later!

CHAPTER 9

Self-Expansion

I was really excited about my gift, yet I never knew when it would be "turned on."

It activated itself when I didn't expect it: during the workshop, at the dinner table with the lady in the red dress, in my back yard after the seminar, on the way to work with the fire hydrant. However, it was noticeably absent when I did expect it: at the gambling tables at Reno, during the following weeks when I expected something to happen, in the restaurant with the waitress...

Following my Reno trip I anxiously awaited the next psychic event, but nothing happened right away. I carefully observed every situation, searching for a repetition of a metaphysical occurrence. Whenever someone began a conversation, I went inside to my "feeling place" and searched for psychic clues to what they might say next. At sporting events I attempted to anticipate a significant occurrence so I could take pleasure in saying, "I knew that was going to happen."

Although disappointed that more paranormal events were not occurring, I was beginning to express my feelings as I'd been encouraged to do at the seminar. In conversations with friends I found that I was stating how I felt instead of routinely agreeing in my usual, accommodating fashion. For the first time in a long time, I was feeling *special.* I was aware of feelings and emotions that I had not observed in years. I was beginning to comprehend that the gifts from the seminar weekend, including the resultant psychic experiences, were about *expanding my being— becoming aware of who I truly am!*

I was also becoming much more aware on multiple levels. For example, I was cognizant of my *peripheral* vision, observing things that would have escaped my notice before. I was increasing my general sense of awareness. Occupying an out-of-the-way corner at social gatherings, I observed with fascination people or events that I had never before bothered noticing.

At a large party I became aware, probably for the first time, that I was also observing *me!* Observing me... this was similar to a motion picture camera receding for a wide-angle shot to comprehend the *entire* action, not just the immediate foreground, and to observe the extended field of vision. Like that camera, I focused on myself as well as the action; I expanded my field of awareness.

I was conscious of just my hands and arms at first, but gradually I gained a sense of my entire body and an increased awareness of *me.* At the same time, I separated "me" from the myriad of other external events occurring beyond my immediate awareness of myself.

This experience of "self," along with the expansion of my previously closed intuitive nature, opened the doors to my natural, God-given psychic or intuitive aptitude and led me to discover that *feelings are the bridge between thinking and truly "being"!*

Reasoning is necessary, of course; yet it was never intended to overpower our feeling nature. Through life programming, many of us have allowed reasoning to isolate us from our feelings, thereby denying us full comprehension of our entire being.

To open to our psychic ability, we must first pay attention to our feelings. By acknowledging our emotional nature, we will begin to expand our awareness.

Once I committed to this path—this expansion of self— my sense of peripheral vision became more acute. I began to "see" things differently. This new way of seeing was a physical manifestation of increased self-awareness and a deeper knowledge of reality. The result was not an increased ego, but a greater knowing of who I was and an entry or graduation into a higher spiritual level.

Psychic attunement begins with an increased awareness of oneself... and an awareness of one's awareness.

Can *you* do it? Remember the old adages "you can do it if you try" and "practice makes perfect" that we've heard for so long? Like most lessons in life, we must discover the truth of these sayings for ourselves. The opportunity for self-discovery will present itself when the timing is right and we are prepared to experience it.

We can also turn it on when we are ready, and the fact that you are reading this book suggests that you are!

Considerable time passed before I learned to accept and work with this gift or even began to understand why I was selected to experience this proficiency of perception.

Then, by "coincidence," I met Gerri Patton, whom you'll meet later in this book. Gerri is a practicing psychic and researcher, among many other things. Her approach to *who* is psychic is unusual. Gerri insists that most psychics either are born with their gift or acquire it as the result of experiencing a life-threatening event, such as an electrical shock or a near-death experience. She adds that if you are born under certain astrological signs, you possess an increased, natural psychic ability, which can be enhanced if you can go beyond the accompanying self-denial.

In my case, my mother told me that when I was about 3 years old, I poked a hairpin into an electrical outlet and received one hell of a shock! (Warning: Kids, do *not* try this!) Although the memory of that shock is vague, Gerri claims that the electrical charge probably altered my physical energy and awoke the psychic ability I later developed.

Be clear: we *all* have intuitive or psychic *ability*. What we call "women's intuition" is a good example of this natural ability. What mother cannot recall an instance when she "knew" that her young child was in danger or she "felt" that some member of her family required her immediate assistance?

In a broad sense, being psychic or intuitive is essentially the same thing. Webster's *New World Dictionary* defines the word psychic as knowing "beyond natural or known physical process." Intuition means "learning something without the consciousness of reasoning."

Many people use their psychic or intuitive skills without realizing it. Some psychics express this notion as being in touch with the right brain versus the left brain. Others speak in terms of *yin* rather than *yang* (pronounced "yan") energy. Women generally have these knowing feelings more easily then men do, perhaps labeling them "feelings" or "intuition." For example, they might know who is on the telephone before answering it, or they might be thinking about their husbands precisely when their mates undergo intense emotional experiences. (*Knowing* that they need a new dress for an upcoming party does *not* count.) An explanation for this is that women are typically *more aware of their feelings* than men are.

Yin and yang are ancient Eastern spiritual concepts which are becoming more accepted in the West. The theory is that *all* things are both male and female energy. At the beginning of time, the cosmos, or "All That Is," in a desire to manifest Itself more fully, divided Its nature into two opposing energies: yin and yang. Yin represents the negative and yang the positive forces within all things, from the protons and electrons of atoms to the conscious and subconscious of the human psyche.

Yin is female, representing the female aspects of nature: compassion, sensitivity, beauty, emotion, creativity, expression and the like. For example, an artist or musician expresses yin energy through the communication of his or her creativity. Yang is male, representing the opposite demeanor of things: survival power, logic, ego, control, strength and so on. A politician or leader, male or female, is displaying yang energy through the use of power and ego. All of us embody both yin and yang energy, but society encourages us to behave according to gender norms and rules.

Therefore, because women in our society are more apt to express their yin energy than men, women are often more in touch with their feelings and sensitivity, and they more easily tap into their psychic resources. Following their natural feminine nature, women access their right brain or creative side and express the passive or yin energy. All of this, of course, is rapidly changing during the late 20th century, regardless of our gender, as we become more comfortable with both our male and female energy.

Men, on the other hand, tend to be more aggressive, ego competitive and logical in their thinking because, if nothing else, they are expected to be. Since men tend to rely more on logic, the typical male of our species is less sensitive (psychic) than the female. Fortunately, this, too, is changing.

FACT: *All people* can use their psychic abilities if they *believe* they possess the ability and if they have the *desire* and assume the *risk*.

Psychic awareness, then, is a means of becoming more aware of *who* we are. One way of doing this is to contact our yin or higher spiritual nature.

Knowing who we are is a first step in becoming all that we can be!

If we want to find our way when we are lost, is it not best to first establish our current location? It follows that to successfully get to where we are going in life, we must first find out *where we are*. Where we are equates to whatever is happening in our life right now. We must recognize our present situation and what we want to change before we can find our new direction with any accuracy.

And that brings us to purpose...

We each have a purpose in this life, and we can fulfill our destiny more easily once we know *what* our life's mission is. Where are we heading? What do we need to accomplish?

To more fully comprehend these questions and the *source* of psychic knowing, we must first consider the spiritual-scientific nature of the universe, as well as our relationship and function within it.

Most philosophers would agree that "in the beginning" there was only energy. In fact, energy is all there is even now.

Modern scientists *also* believe that all things are energy.

Einstein proved that concept with his $E = MC^2$ equation. If we recall our high school physics class, we may remember our teacher explaining that everything is energy. In reality, the chair we sit on or the book we read is not really solid. Because electrons and protons and quarks are doing their "vibration thing," we *perceive* matter to be solid. In fact, if we were to enlarge the nucleus of an atom to the size of a marble, the closest electron would be many miles distant, relatively speaking, with a vast amount of "nothingness" between. Everything is either energy or nothingness. But since we are told all things are energy, nothingness must be something by virtue of just being there. In *The Celestine Prophecy,* James Redfield explains it another way: "The whole of Einstein's work was to show that what we perceive as hard matter is mostly empty space with a pattern of energy running through it."

But "nothingness" is "something" by just being "there."

So… all things are energy. All things have always been and will always be, essentially, just energy. From a spiritual point of view, one might say that in the beginning all energy was ONE energy. Now we can discuss what to call this One Energy; call It God, call It Universal Mind, call It Nature or Source, call It whatever you wish, but most believe this One Energy had—and still has—a direction, purpose or reason for being.

Also, consider that in the beginning, this One Energy had a limited experience of Itself because It was all there was. It couldn't even observe Itself since It had no "place" to distance Itself from Itself. Everything was the same "Oneness."

Some would say that It decided, since It *was* everything, to separate Its *unconsciousness* from Its conscious Self and experience Its unconscious Self separately from the One. Hence, by this process, the universe was "created."

Following this thought process, *we* are individual portions of this Unconsciousness, experiencing Itself, becoming conscious. We are, then, part of the Whole, the Oneness expressing Itself. Or said another way, we are the whole expressing Itself individually!

Consider an analogy of a beach and the grains of sand on that beach. Visualize being in a helicopter, looking down on a beautiful, white, sandy beach—a "beach," a singular noun. One beautiful, quiet and secluded beach. When the helicopter lands, you walk out onto the beach and discover that it actually consists of countless grains of sand that *collectively* make up the beach. Each grain of sand is different, yet not unlike the next. Remove one grain of sand, and it would hardly be missed. Eliminate *all* the grains of sand, and you would have *no* beach.

Oneness or Collective Energy is analogous to the beach, and our individual consciousness is analogous to the grains of sand. Our individual grain of sand is hardly noticeable to the whole, but *there is no other grain any more significant than our one grain.*

The beach is the sum of all of its parts, and no one piece is any more important than the next. God, by this reasoning, is the Collective Whole or All That Is, and each of us is as significant a piece of the Is as any other!

So, continuing this notion, we are a portion of the Source, expressing Himself/Herself/Itself. Each of us is a part of this Collective Whole, each "made in Its image." If this Ultimate Being has a purpose, then *we* have a purpose, and that purpose is to *fully* experience ourselves. Since we are each unique, we each express ourselves individually and differently—all the more reason to fully comprehend who we really are and where we wish to go in order to truly express our individual purpose. Tuning in to our psychic ability assists us in this endeavor.

This Supreme Being has a specific purpose in expressing Itself as us. And, being *All* there is, It is eternal—without beginning or end—so it seems logical that we, too, are eternal. Since we are eternal, why does Western society have such difficulty accepting the concept of reincarnation? Why would one possibly conclude that we have only one shot at this physical existence stuff? Does it make sense that this loving Supreme Intelligence would play favorites by rewarding some of us with easy and comfortable lives and others with poverty and illness? The idea of reincarnation suggests that we repeatedly manifest in physical form to learn, evolve and express ourselves more fully. It's hard to imagine that we could learn all this in just one time around!

My sudden and dramatic psychic unfolding was for a purpose. Being psychic allows me to more fully understand the true nature of things and, in my specific instance, to complete or repay my *karma* from a past life by serving others. Psychic ability is a tool for growth, and it's a tool we can all access.

The idea of karma suggests that the results or efforts of previous physical forms (past lives) are carried forward and that we are accountable for all of our actions in previous existences. The Biblical saying "an eye for an eye, a tooth for a tooth" can be interpreted as expressing the concept of karma. Good deeds bring good rewards; bad deeds result in difficulty. "What goes around, comes around" is another expression of this idea. Karma explains why a compassionate Creator seemingly rewards some and distresses others.

As previously stated, I am certain that *my* psychic gift is for the purpose of enhancing my personal growth by working through my karma. By using it to give a greater amount than I might expect in return, I can pay off my karmic debt more quickly.

How do I know that? Because countless Eastern philosophers, mystics and psychics have provided this insight, and I have received personal self-validation by searching the deep place within where one's own truth is found.

How do *I* help others? By facilitating their discovery of *their* truth, so that *they* might find their personal path to growth, to purpose and to understanding.

What should *you* do with the gift that is inherent in your nature? Ask your spirit guides or higher self!

CHAPTER 10

Spiritual Guidance—The Next Chapter

So, you might ask, just how does one communicate with this mysterious source of psychic knowing. Exactly what is it that one taps into and how are these messages delivered?

Most traditional spiritualists, shamans, prophets and mystics throughout history have claimed their inspiration emanates from a higher or spiritual origin. This source, of course, has differing names, depending on who you are talking to. Some insist on describing the root of this psychic knowing by a religious connotation, such as God or spirit, while others prefer angels or the Universal Mind. Some shamans of indigenous cultures explain that they commune directly with nature spirits—essences of nature, such as animals, trees or the wind. Brazilian healers pay homage to what they refer to as the 12 universal energies and physically manifest their form when healing. Some Eastern seers claim to interpret the movement of the stars, read the patterns in tea leaves or speak through tarot cards.

Whatever the derivation, those who access this psychic field seem to draw information from somewhere or something beyond the reasoning human mind. Not unlike artists or musicians who go beyond the "yang" mind and give free reign to their creative ability, authentic psychics appear to "channel" knowing beyond their limited and finite human ability.

If those with psychic potential can recognize and identify this means of knowing, they can tune into "It" as needed. In reality it doesn't much matter what name you put to It, other than to acknowledge that It emerges beyond personal and physical boundaries.

I call my source my "spirit guides."

You can call yours whatever you like...

Now, you have to understand that I waited until you were well into my story before I broached the subject of spirit guides. I know that most people view the concept with disdain, dismissing it as either pure fantasy or simply a belief held by members of ignorant, primitive societies. Whenever asked how I know the things which I channel during a psychic reading, I usually fit my answer to the degree of disbelief on a person's face. To illustrate what I encounter when describing this source to others, let me share an incident which "coincidentally" occurred during the writing of this section.

Shirl, my second wife and partner for 10 years, and I recently attended a Christmas party given by a fun couple we had only recently met. We recognized that we would know very few of the other guests. By the time we arrived, the festivities were well under way. While Shirl searched out the hostess, I joined a group of four young men who, judging by the multilayered traces of eggnog on their faces, were well into Christmas cheer. It was typical cocktail party conversation; each male attempted to impress the others with grossly exaggerated stories concerning everything from his business accomplishments to his sexual prowess.

When it came my turn to enter into the conversation, I blurted out that I was writing a book on metaphysics. Doing my best to disregard the immediate wave of disbelief and skepticism relating to the subject matter, I said that it was a lighthearted book meant to encourage individuals to open themselves to the psychic capabilities which we all inherently possess.

A long dramatic silence followed.

Three of the original participants in the conversation simultaneously discovered that their cocktail glasses were empty and abruptly departed to remedy the situation. The remaining individual, probably too embarrassed to leave me standing alone, tentatively inquired as to the title of my next chapter.

Momentarily inspired and looking directly at him with all of the self-assurance that a budding writer could muster, I exclaimed, "Probably I'll call it 'The Next Chapter'!"

One did not have to be a psychic to see him beginning to plot his exit!

As I was preparing to extricate myself from this situation, one curious individual on the periphery of our conversation stepped forward and posed a follow-up question, conceivably playing straight man to my flippant response. "From whence did that absolutely 'brilliant' inspiration come?" he inquired.

"From Amy, one of my spirit guides," I shot back, trusting that my higher guidance would provide the words I would need.

The expression on his face showed that he viewed me midway between a curiosity and an outright weirdo.

I share all of this with you to interject one of my early learned concepts: the existence of what I call my spirit guides or higher spiritual guidance. Allow me to introduce you to my guides in the order that I met them.

First, there is Sami, the guide who first made himself known to me and the one who channels through me when I give psychic readings.

The second guide to appear was Joel, the serious and moralistic one, who insists on being classified as "spiritual" rather than "religious."

Next came Amy, my first female guide and the one who continuously encourages me to recognize and love the little boy part of myself. The first time I encountered her, she "appeared" to my left, said "hi," and then immediately asked if she could get back to me... later!

My fourth guide has not made himself/herself fully known to me. He/she seems to be quite powerful, and I sense him/her to be significant. He/she either vibrates at too high a level, or I have not raised my consciousness sufficiently to fully perceive him/her yet.

What are spirit guides?

Guides can be viewed as advanced spiritual helpers, similar to the Biblical image of angels. In numerous incarnations they have "graduated" from their earthbound karmic bonds and the need to reincarnate in limited physical form. Having reached an advanced spiritual level, they agree to help and guide us while we toil on this planet. If it makes you more comfortable, think of them as higher spiritual thought, or as an intermediary between God and what we perceive as "Reality" or even as energy beings who have just received their spiritual teaching degrees and are now ready to instruct us.

I believe we each select our own guides or, if you like, guardian angels *before* our manifestation onto this physical plane. Our choice is dependent upon the specific lesson we wish to learn during this incarnation. These higher spiritual entities only *guide* us, never dictate to or control us, so that we can complete what we have set out to achieve. They know exactly what we require through their direct access to higher spiritual thought.

They basically do three things.

1. They protect us by minimizing our involvement in situations which might hinder our spiritual growth.
2. They guide us by arranging situations and circumstances for purposes that are often beyond our understanding.
3. They access spiritual information and provide us with ideas or inspirations so that we might complete karma more easily.

Many Eastern traditions suggest we each have at least one and as many as seven guides or angels during any one life. The number of guides we each have can vary and depends on what we want to accomplish. Our guides generally remain with us during our entire lifetime, phasing in and out at various times as needed.

Do most people believe in spiritual guides or angels?

Interestingly enough, a *Time Magazine* poll reported in their December 27, 1993, issue that 69 percent of Americans believe in the existence of angels versus 25 percent who do not. Almost 50 percent of those polled believe they have their own guardian angel. Harvard Divinity School and Boston University have accredited courses on angels or guides. There are countless books reporting on the subject and even popular newsletters issued, such as *Angel Watch,* published by Eileen Freeman in New Jersey.

Further, Jewish, Christian, Muslim, Buddhist, Hindu and

Zoroastrian sacred texts often speak of these spiritual beings as messengers or intermediaries between us and the higher Universal Power. Many Catholic children are taught the "Prayer to the Guardian Angel" in their catechism, and Muslims believe angels are present in mosques to record the prayers and testify on Judgment Day.

Winged, angel-like figures appear in ancient Sumerian carvings, as well as on Egyptian tombs, Assyrian reliefs and Catholic cathedrals. Even the well-respected, modern-day theologian Billy Graham wrote a book entitled *Angels: God's Secret Agents*, and the philosopher Mortimer Adler refers to them as "forms of extra-cosmic intelligence."

So, how do we select our own personal guardian angels or spirit guides?

By way of a practical illustration, if we discover we have a medical problem, we consult with the medical specialist most able to help us renew our health. If we have a legal difficulty, we seek legal counsel. The same practicality is true for guides; we bring with us those who can best help us to complete the goals we've set for ourselves for this lifetime.

If you are uncomfortable with the above explanation, consider guides as being that "place" from which ideas or inspirations come, the voice in your head which nags or inspires. Guides also create events and arrange "coincidences" in order that you might have a specific experience.

However, an encounter with them will likely not occur until you believe it is possible and you wish it to happen. You must have both desire and intention.

If you do want to discover your own spiritual helpers, you might begin to accept that they are nearby, perhaps in the room or space alongside you. As highly spiritual enti-

ties, they vibrate at a much higher frequency than we do in
our physical form. To begin, simply imagine the rate of
their vibrations slowing down, not unlike dust settling after
a windstorm or a tuning fork subsiding after it has been set
into motion.

As you focus on lowering their vibratory rate or density, detect, if you can, the subtle change in the energy in
your immediate vicinity. Become more aware of the "space"
around you, as the essence of your spirit guide's loving and
protective energy surrounds and embraces you. You may
see it as a collective energy or several differing ones. Let
loose of any preconceived ideas or expectations of success
or failure; instead, just be with the process. Identify and
focus on the specific area in your immediate environment
that "feels" different, yet peaceful and familiar.

It is difficult to sense this spiritual essence until you
seriously make the commitment to this process of discovery and exploration. It is not unlike meeting new friends;
the more you sincerely desire to know them, the greater
the opportunity for a complete and lasting bond. Eventually, as you become more practiced in recognizing and discerning subtle energy manifestations, you will begin to perceive your higher guidance in terms of appearances and
individual personalities.

As you sense a recognizable identity, you will begin to
understand its perceived form and intention. A guide resembling a Roman gladiator, for example, suggests a different task and purpose than a graceful ballet dancer. As
you do when analyzing a dream, ask yourself what is unique
about your guide. Then seek to understand why the spiritual energy created the specific form that it did.

During a psychic reading, my clients often begin to sense
their guides at the moment I begin to describe their physical
appearance. They will imagine/see them, even discerning

specific details—the length of their hair or the color of their clothing—seconds before I describe them.

The purpose of initiating contact is, of course, so that my clients can establish their relationship with their guides in order to understand their own truth.

Often the *names* of my clients' guides are *not* revealed to me during a reading. I have learned that if clients seek this knowledge on their own, they are able to establish a stronger, more personal bond. Like everything else, the more interest and effort we invest in connecting and communicating with our guides, the more rewarding the result and the more valuable our guides become.

I am frequently asked how I discovered the names of *my* guides. I once asked the same question of an accomplished psychic friend, Rhoda, admitting to her that I did not know the names of mine. I remember her amazement at my ignorance. "You don't know the names of your guides?" I felt like saying if I knew their names I wouldn't have asked, but I bit my tongue. "No," I politely responded. "I do not."

She leaned over to me and in a low, suggestive voice said, "Then why don't you ask them?"

So... I did... and they promptly told me... *what a simple solution!*

You see, basically, guides are here to help us! They are here for *us* when *we* need them, even if we are not aware of their existence. They are here to give us a nudge when we need one, whether we comprehend this or not. They are here to serve us, even though we may deny that they exist at all.

What could be better than that?

The more we acknowledge them, believe in them or even believe that they *could* exist at all, the more we will be conscious of their actions. Since they are here for *us*, at *our* direction, to serve *our* needs, why not be receptive to them? If we made an agreement to support a friend and then he or she ignored our assistance, wouldn't we become less enthusiastic? Fortunately for us, our guides have more patience!

Since they have access to all the secret spiritual stuff, shouldn't we pay attention to them when they speak?

And when we learn how to pay attention, we will hear responses to questions we want answered!

Have you ever observed young children talking to their invisible playmates—their guides? Listen to the children's dialogue with their imaginary friends and you will recognize that they really believe those friends exist. Children accept the idea that they are talking to invisible beings who become part of *their* reality. Their reality, therefore, results from their belief system.

Change your beliefs and you change your reality!

Children quite often see the truth more clearly than adults do. As kids begin to mature, they lose their individuality and begin to conform to their culture's conditioning. When this happens, a portion of their unique individuality is lost in the process. They lose their inherent knowledge of truth.

As a teenager, I performed magic tricks for a hobby and for extra money. Magicians will tell you that it's *much* easier to fool an adult than a child. Children cannot be misdirected as easily. Since they are recent arrivals to this earth plane of existence, they have not had time to accumulate the many and varied false beliefs we adults use to validate and sustain our egos. They do not buy into the collective logic, predetermined ideas and expectations which adults have been conditioned to accept and which are required to make the desired magical illusion successful.

In fact, small children perceive *their* reality with greater accuracy than their parents do. Children understand their basic truth.

And these "truths" sometimes actually talk to them.

And these truths can be called guides!

More about this later...

CHAPTER 11

Looking for a Teacher

S o... returning to my story, months went by with my newly discovered "gift" unopened. I didn't understand what was physically happening, and few people I knew could help me comprehend what to do about it. I was fairly certain that none of my personal acquaintances were even slightly familiar with psychic phenomena. I sensed that if I did not develop an understanding of what was happening to me, the benefits of my breakthrough might be lost through in-activity. I was definitely concerned.

No sooner had I made the commitment to obtain more knowledge on this subject than a catalog of the spring classes offered at nearby John F. Kennedy University mysteriously "appeared" in my mailbox. Although the bulky package was addressed to me, I couldn't imagine how it had come into my possession, particularly when I inquired at the university and learned that they only mailed catalogs to those re-questing them.

I clearly recall that as I laid the mail on my desk, the catalog "coincidentally" flipped open to the list of classes offered by the Parapsychology Department. Wasn't it interesting, I remember thinking, that the catalog would arrive at this specific time in my life and that my eye would catch the very department that might provide a solution to my current need?

Then, "coincidentally" again, I had a business meeting late in the afternoon the next week near the university. Too late to fight the traffic back to my office, I decided to go there and find out how I might enroll in classes on paranormal experiences.

I parked my car and followed the signs leading to the administration building. The frenzied environment of confused, milling students suggested that I had arrived during the final days of class registration.

While pondering what action to take, I encountered a young man who had taken classes in the Parapsychology Department. After patiently listening to a capsulized version of my predicament, he suggested that I audit a lower division class on psychic phenomena. Pointing out an introductory course that was available to the community at large, he directed me to the proper registration line, cautioning me that the class was popular and was likely to be filled by this late date.

When I arrived at the front of the queue, I opened the catalog and pointed to the class, asking if there were any openings.

The expression on the lady's face behind the counter was doubtful as she consulted her computer. "Oh no," she muttered, "I'm certain this class filled days ago." Then, blinking her eyes in disbelief, she peered over her screen and informed me that there *was* a seat remaining in the class after all. I nodded my acceptance as she quickly completed the enrollment.

As I walked away from the counter, I overheard the same lady inform the student behind me that she was sorry, but the last remaining space in the class he requested had just been filled by the "older fellow" in front of him.

Not only had a series of synchronistic events brought me to the proper location, but I had "created" an opening in the needed class.

I was to learn that this creative process continuously serves us all, whether we are aware of it or not. Most of us know about the laws of physics. Well, it turns out that the continuous process of "creating our individual reality" is a basic law of *meta*physics.

This metaphysical law says that each of us is an individual energy unit expressing itself in physical form and creating our individual experience of reality. Since we each possess our own belief system, each of us experiences life differently. What is pleasurable for one person is agony for another; two people experience identical events in different ways.

Scripture states that in the beginning "the word was made flesh," which is to say that what God thought, God created. Since most will agree that God-The-Creator is love and purpose, and since we are told that we were created in His image, it follows, then, that we just might have the ability to *create* our life experiences by way of our *thinking*. Our thoughts are energy, and this energy manifests itself into form, which we experience as our own individual reality.

Expanding on this natural metaphysical law, we manifest our own reality with each thought. The universe, following the flow of least resistance, much like a mountain stream that takes the easiest course available to it, manifests our reality from the flow of our *thought* energy. Wishing only to please us, it creates what we individually think or believe, thus providing us with the experience it believes we have requested. After all, it is only providing what it thinks we think we want!

Our thoughts lead to our perception, and our perception becomes our reality.

Positive affirmations provide positive results. Likewise, worry and fear, if retained, manifest negative events to support our negative thought process. Richard Bach, author of *Jonathan Livingston Seagull*, wrote a book titled *Illusions*. In this book there is a wonderful phrase illustrating this concept. He writes: "Believe in your limitations and they are yours."

So, if we were to stop worrying, stop creating limitations…

In my life adventure, I was clearly creating the means to obtain the life experiences and answers I needed. Whether I recognized or understood what I had created was a separate issue; what I had created was the means for discovering my truth. Whether I followed the clues or not, that was up to me.

That's what free will is all about!

My class met Tuesday nights for three hours, and I was enthralled from the get-go! Since I was only auditing the course, I felt free to focus on what I found useful to me rather than on what I expected to find on the midterm and final.

Toward the end of the semester, we were treated to a

guest lecturer by the name of Gerri Patton, who fascinated me from the instant she began to speak. Gerri was a practicing psychic and an author, lecturer, researcher, scientist and a genuine character. Besides Susan, the woman who led me through the restaurant experience, Gerri was the only other authentic psychic I had ever met in person. Gerri did *not* fit my preconceived notion of what a psychic was supposed to look like—no crystal ball, no turban and shawl with the little glittering stars.

Asked to speak on how she became a practicing psychic, she told of her near-death experience while undergoing surgery years before. After regaining consciousness, Gerri found she was able to describe specific details of her operation, much to the amazement of the recovery room nurses. Suddenly and unexpectedly, she was aware of things that logically she shouldn't know. In one instance, she confided, she even knew about a secret affair one of her nurses was having with a doctor. (Her later research confirmed that many survivors of near-death experiences become extraordinarily psychic.)

I was struck with our similarity! We both had developed unexpected psychic awareness following a major confrontation with our emotions as middle-aged adults. We both had been confused, fearful and frustrated by what had occurred. In addition, we both were Tauruses and had experienced an electrical shock in our youth!

Near the end of her lecture, she agreed to demonstrate what she called "social readings." She requested that we each shake our hands and hold them in the air, palms inward and fingers extended toward the ceiling. She circulated through the room, providing brief readings to a dozen or so randomly selected students by reading the *backs* of their hands.

She briefly glanced at my hands as she passed my desk

and then suddenly stopped, as if mulling over a thought.

"I'd like to see you after class!" she said to me in her deep voice, her finger waggling in my direction.

Now, my experience has been that whenever one is instructed to remain after class by the teacher, it is seldom good news. Meekly I responded that I was just auditing the class and was not a "real" student; she just shrugged and went on with her readings.

At the completion of the lecture and after all the other students had left, I walked to her desk as she began to pack up her notes. She looked up, a serious look on her face, and informed me that she had "seen" that I was *very* psychic. She declared that I must honor this gift I had been given!

I began to briefly relate the story of what had brought me to this class. Waving off my explanation in mid-sentence, she said I must immediately learn all I could about this phenomenon. She warned me if I did not begin to use it properly, I might lose the gift entirely.

After about five minutes, she wound down her flow of words and finished gathering her notes together, indicating that our one-way conversation had ended. Then, abruptly pausing in mid-stride on her way to the door, she grabbed my arm. Her eyes darted to a corner of the ceiling as if acknowledging the source of her thought. (The corner of the ceiling, *déjà vu*, Susan's guides hung out there, too!)

"Every few years or so, I teach a few students how to develop their psychic ability," she reported, her voice gentle, "and *you* might want to think about joining my palmistry class."

She stared at me as if waiting for an immediate commitment. Although fascinated and mesmerized, a palmistry class was not quite what I had in mind. Not having a ready response, I fumbled with a request for her phone number, suggesting that I would get back to her.

"No problem," she responded, shifting the materials she was carrying from one hand to the other. "I'll save you a place."

I thought about Gerri often during the next several days. I realized that I had finally located someone who could provide me clarity and direction. After much deliberation, I called her to inquire about fees and dates.

She stated her rates and defined the hours and duration of her classes.

I expressed that I really wasn't interested in palmistry, my mind shifting to one of those 1940s movie scenes of a Gypsy fortune teller with the large hand out in front of the tent.

Gerri patiently informed me that although being psychic was a spiritual gift, much like being artistic was a creative gift, psychics often used a "tool" to focus their work. She explained that many psychics were palmists or tarot card readers. Others worked with astrology, numerology or channeled spirit guides. She even had a psychic friend who claimed that she channeled information from her cat.

"I use palmistry and psychometry," she explained, defining psychometry as the practice of reading vibrations from a hand-held object.

She explained that it made no difference to her which tool I used. "If it works, go with it," she added with certainty.

I hesitated. Did I wish to commit time and money to someone I hardly knew, particularly someone whose close friend held frequent conversations with her cat?

I asked if she could "guarantee" to make me psychic.

"The only thing I can guarantee you is death and taxes," she responded with a laugh, explaining that she would teach me an ancient craft used successfully by psychics for thousands of years. She promised that after I completed her instruction, I would have a valuable tool, one that would be as useful to me as a musical instrument is to a musician who plays it when creating music.

I decided to go for it!

CHAPTER 12

Developing a Focus

I was astounded to discover that the ancient method of "reading" hands was not only possible, but accurate! Gerri taught us to discern personal character traits in the various lines and mounds displayed in the palms of our hands. The length and shape of the fingers and how we hold them relative to one another suggest additional pieces of information.

I learned that the information stamped in each hand differs. The markings in our dominant hand signify our present day, individual personality, while our passive hand provides insight into the issues that we are to resolve in this life. I have since concluded that our second hand also reveals who we have been in the most recent incarnations, since our present life continues to work through the karma and issues of our past lives.

A good psychic palmist is one who successfully combines the knowledge of this age-old, well-tested tradition of hand interpretation with intuitive or psychic sense. Reading a palm is not unlike reading a map—you select several highways that will lead you to your destination, and then you allow your intuitive "knowing" to designate the particular route that will best serve your needs.

A reputable palmist will *never* tell you which course to follow. Instead, he or she will "channel" information from higher spiritual levels that you might not be able to reach on your own. A valid psychic only provides you information that you already possess, hidden in the deep recesses of your unconsciousness—knowledge repressed or forgotten.

Legitimate palmists do not predict the future as I had naively assumed. Instead, authentic seers present information to assist in the growth of their clients. The Hollywood stereotype of a psychic peering into your hand and stating that you are going to meet a tall, dark stranger is movie fiction. Instead, a psychic might provide clues to the type of mate most compatible with someone's needs.

Most importantly, in studying palmistry I became more convinced that we are *all* psychic in one manner or another. True intuitive knowing *begins* with focus, and palmistry is but one of many methods for focusing. For example, if your most accurate means of perception is envisioning an event in your mind's eye, you are most likely to receive messages clairvoyantly. If, on the other hand, you learn or remember best by hearing sounds, you most likely can expand your natural clairaudient talents.

Each week between classes, Gerri encouraged us to "read" the public, using the information taught the week before. I found myself staying up until all hours of the morning observing the late-night talk shows and scrutinizing the guests as they gestured with their hands.

During the week, I would visit the restaurant across the street from my office, and, in exchange for their feedback, I'd read people who had learned about my psychic ability.

Late lunch patrons who curiously observed waitresses shaking their hands and holding them up in the air as they paused at my table would often become my next free clients. This was a wonderful method of obtaining validation while building my much-needed confidence.

I found that by looking at someone's hands, I could "read" a personality trait if I followed the guidelines that Gerri taught. When my subject would invariably say, *"How did you know that?"* I would confidently "expand" on what the lines and mounds suggested and speak from a more intuitive or psychic level.

And when they would exclaim, "How did you know *that?"* I would do my best to mask my ecstatic and delirious ebullition by calmly going on to another line in the hand with all the straight-faced, professional style I could muster. This procedure allowed me to gradually confirm my yet untrained psychic ability.

As we students gathered before each palmistry class, we shared the progress and failures we each had experienced during the past week. Although we were all using Gerri's method, it became apparent that only a few of us were actually going beyond her instruction and reading intuitively.

One evening as I was leaving the class, Gerri motioned for me to remain. She gave me a brief reading, accurately listing in precise detail specific struggles that I was encountering in my personal life at that time. She informed me that she had detected some major directional changes I was about to encounter, and that my psychic skills were surfacing to enhance my personal growth.

What was about to happen? I wanted to know more about the important transformations she had detailed. She informed me that psychics do not really "see the future" as if it were preordained in a set script; instead, they suggest the *potential* of what might take place, if the course of the present energy is unalterably extended beyond the present time.

She was attempting to explain a concept that many on the path to full awareness struggle to understand. This idea concerns a metaphysical notion that both "time" and "space" exist *only* in the limited arena we call the physical world, but not in what might be labeled "true reality."

The physical existence each of us experiences is called an "illusion" by avatars, gurus and other planetary enlightened ones. They explain that what we call "reality" is, "in Reality," an "illusion" since each of us has separate and differing perceptions of how we experience it. As suggested in the previous chapter, each of us creates our own reality—based on our individual understanding—through the simple act of *interpreting* what we think and perceive our experiences to be.

As an example of this concept, I remember my father feeling fulfillment when someone asked him to repair a broken object. He had a full assortment of tools, understood how to use them all, and he enjoyed figuring out and fixing things.

I, on the other hand, consider it a chore to make any repair. I do not have the required patience, and I can virtually guarantee that Murphy's Law (anything that can go wrong, will!) will be fully in effect the moment I try to fix something.

As illustrated, one man's work is another man's pleasure... two people experiencing the same situation will often experience it quite differently.

Reality is, then, how we perceive it!

Scientists would logically explain that the reason we each experience things dissimilarly is that we physically *see* things differently. When we focus on an object, our eyes transmit electrochemical impulses to our brains which, with assistance from our nervous systems, *interpret* them as thought patterns. As the object on which we concentrate becomes predominant in our minds, our brains minimize what they deem less important, thereby further altering what is viewed.

Mystics, on the other hand, conclude that our perception is controlled by what we *believe*. They would suggest that if we observe an individual we *believe* to be a threat, we "see" a threatening person. Since we all interpret according to our own experiences, conditioning and beliefs, the mystics feel that we each arrive at different conclusions regarding the object observed.

Both the Western and Eastern points of view conclude that we cannot agree on what is. Our perceived reality becomes, then, an illusion!

Time is an illusion as well, although this is a bit more difficult to explain!

Astronomers have recently discovered what they are convinced is a glimpse of the universe at the *actual moment* of conception, which occurred approximately 15 billion years ago, give or take a millennium. Although they are all in basic agreement as to the amount of time which has occurred *since* the event, quantum physics suggests that events occurring *earlier* than this moment are not measurable, and therefore are *nonexistent time-wise and space-wise.*

Prior to the "Big Bang," the sum total of all form and existence was contained in a dense object *smaller* than a single electron. For this reason, today's accepted rules relating to time and space did not come into being until *after* a "time" when matter expanded and the entire universe began to obey the laws of quantum mechanics. These laws state that space and time were once one and the same. A modern physicist even flippantly referred to the relationship of space and time as having an inherent, fine-scale "clumpiness."

Admittedly, all of this is somewhat confusing and overly simplified. Nonetheless, scientific types have concluded from this mumbo jumbo that time exists *only* in physical form; it is the fourth dimension following length, width and depth. The only aspect of time that is real, they reason, is the "now," since existence is really nothing more than a continuous series of "moments of now."

As a child in Sunday School, I was always fascinated with the ideas that "God created everything" and "God always was." Since I'd been led to believe that everything has to have a location and a beginning, I wondered what was God just *before* He was? If God started on, say, a Monday at 8:30 A.M., then how did He get there... who created Him... and what existed the day before?

"But God always was" had been the clergyman's response, providing me with no further insight. Given my childhood understanding of reality and my acceptance of time as separate, measured events, one following another, the clergyman's response made no sense.

Our *concept* of time is limited, and until we cast off this limitation, our understanding and experience will remain limited!

To further confuse things, quantum physicists state that time is a "notion." It really doesn't exist at all! They explain that time is relative to how we experience sensory change. For example, if we are doing something we truly enjoy, time passes quickly. If we are involved in something we do not like, time slows down; it seems to last forever. If we are rushed, we seem to run out of time, as if it were something we possessed. And when our consciousness comes to a standstill, as happens in the special moment that the quantum folks call Unity Consciousness, or spiritualists label a religious experience, then time *doesn't exist at all!*

If it is difficult to accept that time doesn't exist at all, then how about considering that time exists only as we *perceive* it within the *illusion* of the physical plane or while we remain separated from God-consciousness.

The enlightened ones speak of God as eternal, forever, infinite. They tell us that the closer we get to God-consciousness, the less time becomes a factor. Time, by their reasoning, is similar to infinity. Like God or space, time has no limitation and, therefore, does not exist as the limited measurement we have previously assumed it to be.

In Richard Bach's novel titled *ONE,* he illustrates a fascinating idea regarding time. This book suggests that when people make major shifts in their lives, essences or pieces of them continue experiencing life as if it hasn't changed. Those who accept this viewpoint conceive that we are involved in many parallel life experiences, all experiencing ourselves individually yet simultaneously.

Some theorists suggest that if UFOs are, indeed, spaceships, they must be powered by antimatter fuel, which reacts to positive matter by distorting both time and space. This distortion allows the spacecraft to cover vast "distances" in a reasonable "length of time." Otherwise, because it is theoretically impossible to exceed the speed of light, it would take many lifetimes to cover the distances we know separate the galaxies.

When a psychic sees the future, he or she sees only one of the possible options, and that's the point that is being made here. We each have free will, and we can change our minds at any "time."

Change our perception and we change our reality!

Therefore, by the above logic, future events are *probable*. Borrowing Richard Bach's idea, any future event is merely one of many possibilities you *may* experience in *one* of your realities (and realities are *illusions,* which, as mentioned earlier, is the title of one of his books).

If you're still with me, consider one more concept: psychics "remember" the future. If *all* that we experience is the continuous "moment of now," then a future event, which hasn't physically happened yet, must somehow be occurring in the moment of now. But since we are *not* perceiving that we are experiencing it in our present moment, we then must be *remembering* it, as we do with past events.

The point is that reality and time just may be different from the concepts we were taught... and, as we cruise through life, we discover that many teachings we once held as true are *not* true. These presumed truthful suppositions, which once formed the basis for our false beliefs, fall away— no longer valid parts of our reality—concepts such as:

... If you don't see it, it doesn't exist... or

... Psychic experiences don't exist because the one measuring the events can't prove them or hasn't experienced them personally... or

... Something isn't really hiding under your bed when you *know* that it is!

CHAPTER 13

Going Public

I had no sooner completed the palmistry class than I received a phone call from Gerri, inviting me to a special party. She described the evening as a charity event intended to raise money for a local cause. It would take place at a private estate in an exclusive San Francisco Bay Area suburb. The tickets were priced at $75, the attire was formal and she would be pleased if I would attend.

Now, you have to believe that I was extremely flattered that she asked me, but I was not about to get all gussied up and spend $150 a couple to attend a stuffy charity event, particularly since I wasn't likely to know anyone else there. I responded by telling Gerri that I really appreciated the invitation but had conflicting plans for that evening.

Persistently, she suggested that I might want to reconsider my plans, that this would be a wonderful opportunity to meet many of her well-known psychic friends whom she had personally invited. As Gerri described the party format, I learned that most of the guests would receive personalized psychic readings. She was emphatic that this was an opportunity I would not want to miss.

I replied that I would see what I could do about changing my plans. As the conversation ended, she rejoined that she would expect to hear from me within the week. I thought it quite strange that she was requesting my response so soon since the party was more than a month away.

Several days later she called again, inquiring if I had made up my mind. Assuming that she probably had several extra tickets she was concerned about unloading, I questioned her as to why she was so insistent on an answer this early.

"Because," she patiently explained, "I have printing deadlines, and I must know whether or not to include your name in the list of psychics for the program!"

"Gulp... " Gerri was inviting *me* to be one of the psychics!

It was difficult to hear the remaining portion of the conversation because of the loud thumping sound my heart made in my eardrums. Inanely, I mumbled something about water overflowing in my bathtub and assured her that I would get back to her later that evening.

After taking time to collect my thoughts, I called her, calmly informing her that while I really appreciated her considering *me* for this illustrious gathering, I certainly did *not* include myself in that league!

Gerri quickly came back with, "You are one of the best students I ever had," as well as, "This is a chance of a lifetime" and "You can do it." She tossed a few additional clichés at me, including, "If you really required proof, this is your chance." Then switching moods, she confided, "Plus the fact, I want to show you off!"

While my mind was actively forming the words, "Thanks for thinking of me but... ," I found my mouth instead blurting out, "Yes, I'll be there... and thank you!"

After the call I remember thinking that my guides might have overstepped their bounds in pushing me into psychic readings at a public function before I was ready! I certainly did not feel qualified or prepared. What if *they* did not show up that evening?... it was *I* who would be embarrassed, not them.

On the night of the big event, as I parked my car in front of a swank mansion set well back from the street, I was still uncertain about my risky and potentially disastrous predicament. I felt quite insignificant walking through the massive wrought iron gates into a stately, well-manicured garden, complete with ponds and a picturesque gazebo. As I approached the entry, I noted one of those iron statues to which I could have tied my horse-drawn carriage, had I arrived in one.

Gerri had invited 15 psychics, many of them well-known. Warmly welcoming us, she instantly made us feel comfortable, introducing those of us who did not know each other. Although there were definitely a few large egos present, everyone was generally accepting of me, the new kid on the block.

The hostess in charge of the evening's activities carefully explained the ground rules. Each of us would do our readings in a separate room in the huge, three-story mansion. We were free to pick our own location. We would each be expected to read about a dozen people in three to four hours, the guests being ushered to us every 15 to 20 minutes.

She finished her instructions with the encouragement to have fun, adding, "Just give my guests positive statements and please try not to upset any of them. Remember many of them do not believe in this psychic stuff."

Following her directions, we each set out to explore this enormous home and find our own individual place to "do our psychic stuff." The hostess had set aside eight bedrooms, two dens, an office, a study and several other rooms whose functions were less clear. She even included the quaint, fully stocked wine cellar in the basement.

I climbed the grand stairway to the third floor and peered into the bedrooms to find the one that "felt" the best to me. As I entered one beautifully decorated bedroom at the end of the hall, I was overwhelmed with nausea and could hardly breathe. I quickly backed out of this stifling room, closed the door and selected another bedroom at the opposite end of the hall where I felt more at ease, though still not terribly secure about what I was doing there in the first place.

After rearranging the table and chairs into positions that felt the most comfortable, I scattered a few of my favorite crystals about the room. I cleansed it by imagining a white light emanating from the center of my body and becoming larger and brighter, sweeping the room clean of any possible negative vibes which might be lingering there. (I had learned this simple technique during a workshop attended with the group who had initially introduced me to the idea of spirit guides.)

When my little ceremony was complete, I departed the room to join the others who were reassembling in the living room on the main floor. As I started for the stairs, I noticed a woman psychic frozen in the doorway of the bedroom where I'd felt extreme discomfort only minutes before. Her distressed look indicated that she was in touch with the same force I had encountered. I instinctively started toward her as if drawn to an unexplainable magnetism.

"Something evil has taken place in there," she exclaimed in a low, trembling voice before I could ask the obvious question. "There are negative forces in that room." As I was about to tell her that I'd experienced a similar sensation earlier in that room, Gerri came bounding up the stairs, intent on making sure that all her charges were comfortably situated.

"What's wrong?" she shouted from the end of the hall, reacting to our body language and our frightened expressions.

"Have you been in *there?*" I asked meekly, pointing to the small space that was having a major affect on both the woman and myself. I thought, if anyone would sense the negative energy in that room, Gerri would.

She looked at us both and began laughing. "No way," she said, "not *that* room. That's where the murder took place... it's creepy in there!"

As we stood in the hall, our conversation attracted others on their return downstairs. I was surprised to learn that the majority of psychics who had explored this portion of the house had felt equally uncomfortable when entering that specific room!

That room remained empty for the remainder of the night!

The evening turned out very well. As it happened, each guest experienced several psychic readings. Many who previously thought that psychic readings were suspect at best were believers by the end of the evening.

During readings, I found I could always determine if I was reading clients accurately because first-timers would generally begin to squirm and ask, "How did you know that?" Then they invariably began to look nervously about the room as if searching for a hidden camera recording their responses. Those who felt more comfortable with the process would say, *"Funny you should say that...,"* pause, then go on to share intimate details they probably would not confide to their closest friends.

As the evening came to a close, I finally accepted that I was truly psychic. Under rather difficult conditions I had experienced my baptism into the world of public readings. Gerri had previously suggested in class that her students conduct a minimum of 100 readings before they could truly consider themselves credible psychics. Although I had yet to complete the 100 readings, I felt that on this night I had earned my diploma!

CHAPTER 14

Beyond the Physical World

The impact of entering the room where the murder had taken place remained with me long after the readings at the charity function. I was still perplexed about *what* I had experienced and, perhaps equally significantly, *why*. Entering the room, I'd definitely had a depressing and suffocating feeling. Had I sensed a ghost? Had an evil or negative energy remained after the murder? Without question, I had encountered something, and I was driven to learn more.

By "coincidence" (that word again), I gained much-needed insight at a spiritual weekend retreat several months later. The setting was a remote resort community, and those attending, for the most part, sought spiritual wisdom beyond that provided by conventional religion.

Here I met others who had paranormal experiences, from near-death encounters to communication with the spirit realm. Because in this weekend environment we were safe from the ridicule we might have experienced elsewhere, many of us stayed up long into the night relating our personal encounters with the unknown.

One woman I shall call Carolyn related a fascinating story about her near-death experience and what she remembered of the "other side." She had recently been seriously injured in an auto accident and "woke up" in the hospital operating room at the very moment she was pronounced clinically dead!

Quite lucid, not realizing what was taking place, she began asking questions of the nurses around her. No one seemed to have the time to answer, as if preoccupied by a greater concern. She then felt her body slip off the operating table in the direction of her feet and unexplainably begin to float in the air, yet no one seemed to notice.

Carolyn gently floated six to eight feet above the table, where she hovered while observing the commotion throughout the room. One orderly dropped something round on the floor, swore and chased it to the corner of the room. A nurse described in detail a bedspread she had recently purchased for her daughter's room, including how much it cost and how well it blended with the drapes.

Then Carolyn noticed a body on the table. It was her own! Her body was lying motionless and covered with blood!

As she continued to float, she calmly noticed that her consciousness was contained in some kind of shimmery transparent body, which, for some reason, did not feel the least bit foreign. When she refocused her eyes, she became aware of a tunnel above her in the distance. Drawn to its entrance, she felt no hesitancy in entering. Then, exiting into a beautifully peaceful meadow, she was immersed in soft, soothing music and an incredibly peaceful white light. Carolyn recounted in detail that she floated and swam for an indeterminate period in this light space, experiencing sensations unlike any other she had ever encountered. It was intensely bright, but it did not hurt her eyes to look into it. She declared that the entire experience was exquisitely wonderful!

When I asked for more details, her response was that words were simply inadequate. She could only report that she did not see or hear as she had ever done before.

After a long "time," although Carolyn was quick to say that time did not seem to exist, she came upon a wide river which she could not cross. On the other side, all she could see was an indescribably loving face. She could not discern gender, nor could she remember if the face had a body because her entire attention was drawn to the loving, compassionate eyes.

The face lovingly expressed telepathically to her that she had to "go back... return to her physical body." She heard "go back" echoing over and over in her head, as she felt herself being tugged in the opposite direction. The next thing she recalled was that she was lying in an unfamiliar hospital room in a great deal of pain.

When she regained enough strength to speak, she told anyone who would listen about the wonders of her adventure and her specific recollections in the operating room.

Not surprisingly, Carolyn could not find anyone who believed her.

Later, and only after persistent questioning, Carolyn found that she had been pronounced dead for several minutes. She discovered that many of the details she observed during the operation actually occurred, including the dropped object and the conversation about the bedspread. Everyone remained doubtful of her story, however, convinced that someone had told her what had happened during the time of her "death."

After a week of severe pain and the realization that her body would be permanently deformed, Carolyn removed the life supports from her own body. She desired to return to the peace she knew existed beyond death.

This time she went straight to the face—no tunnel, no lightness, no beautiful music. The face was still loving and compassionate, yet wore a stern, disapproving expression. The face looked deep into her soul and spoke telepathically to her heart. "You must go back; you are not finished!"

Carolyn said it was then that she instantly understood why she had to return to the physical plane. It was not an intellectual knowing; it was a deep, unchallengeable recognition of the purpose of life and her specific role in its unfolding drama.

Naturally, the experience had a profound, radical effect on her! So much so that she healed quickly and, upon release from the hospital, immediately changed careers to counsel the dying. She felt compelled to share with whoever would listen a report of her experience of the heavenly place she *knew* existed after death.

If dying was such a wondrous experience, I asked her, why did I experience such negative feelings the night of the charity party in the mansion bedroom where the grisly death had taken place?

She responded that, first, when someone takes another's life, violent energies attach to the physical plane and can often be perceived by those who have opened their psychic channels.

I asked her what a second reason might be.

"Ghosts," she shrugged, her serious expression giving way to a smile as she noted my reaction.

Ghosts, she explained, are the spiritual remains of people who have died but, for one reason or another, have not entirely departed the physical realm. Often they don't realize they have died, particularly if their death is sudden or unexpected. They may also remain connected to the earth plane if someone depends on them, such as a small child.

"And," she added as if an afterthought, "sometimes they are just lost!"

She restated that ghosts are very often perceived by people who have opened their sixth chakra, or third eye, and recommended several books on the subject.

This understanding was crucial to my encounter with several ghosts in Europe.

CHAPTER 15

Things That Go Bump in the Night

My next experience with ghosts occurred some years later while traveling along the historic Rhine River region in Germany.

While Shirl and I were vacationing through Europe, we managed to obtain an invitation to tour one of the old, ghostly, privately owned castles overlooking the historic Rhine River... at night!

It was a picturesque fortress, a somber sentinel perched on a mountain top overlooking the river. Complete with a moat, drawbridge and all the trimmings, it was a classic, storybook castle. To add to the drama, we arrived to the sound of echoing thunder claps, with the full moon peeking out at us from behind dark, ominous clouds!

Responding to the large and loud brass knockers mounted on the massive wooden doors, our host greeted us warmly and welcomed us inside. Dressed in modern garb, he seemed out of place in the midst of past-century sur-

roundings. He graciously ushered us into a waiting room—
a medieval space with authentic suits of armor and swords
like those in a well-stocked European museum. The enormous scale of the room completely dwarfed us.

When he left to greet a few other guests, we felt sus-
pended in a momentary, incredible time warp, and I think
neither of us would have been surprised to see one of the
three Musketeers come swashbuckling into the room.

Presently, our host led the assembled participants on
an exciting adventure through this cavernous edifice, en-
couraging us to explore freely. Torches mounted on the
walls of the windowless passageways lighted our way.

Pausing in a room at the very top of one of the towers,
our castle guide spoke in detail of the castle's history and a
few of its more colorful occupants. He also spoke briefly
about the medieval folklore of the region and several other
castles in which he lived while researching their chronology.

When someone flippantly asked if he had ever encountered ghosts in any of these ancient structures, he paused,
as if to carefully consider his answer.

"A few," he said with a slight smile lighting his naturally
grave expression.

"Seen any ghosts in *this* castle?" asked a rather stout
woman, unable to disguise a nervous laugh as she looked
at the rest of us for support. Our guide's eyes narrowed.

"Matter of fact, I have," he answered after a long pause,
his voice lowered in unmistakable seriousness.

To everyone's fascination, he described the resident
aberration, an old man most often observed in the upper
portion of the citadel near where we were now standing.
With a wry chuckle, he finished by requesting that we immediately inform him of any sightings.

Sometime later, as we made our way to a winding, stone
staircase to return to the main level far below, I told our

intriguing leader that I was a professional psychic and that, although I did not see his ghost in the topmost room, I definitely felt a disturbing presence in one of the lower bedrooms visited earlier.

"Europe's certainly the place to see them," he commented, "particularly in and around old, historic buildings and castles along the Rhine. Seen any other ghosts while in Europe?"

"Funny you should ask," I returned, excited to report a recent spooky confrontation Shirl and I had encountered only weeks before in London. I briefly recounted how we had befriended an innkeeper of a well-known "haunted" pub.

We had learned from several locals that whenever a specific basement door between two separate storage areas in the lower level of this tavern was closed for the night, mysterious, unexplainable events would often take place. Some weeks before we arrived, for example, several cases of beer had been overturned and scattered about, and many bottles had been broken. Since the only passage in and out of the basement was through a bolted door in his private residential quarters, the new owner was beginning to believe the ghostly rumors, which had chased away the previous owners.

After some prompting, the innkeeper permitted us to explore. Grabbing a flashlight, he led us down a rickety, old wooden stairway to the subterranean vault under the pub proper. As we entered the storeroom where the nocturnal activity had occasionally taken place, the air grew heavy. We could easily sense that this was a place of suffering and death!

The new tavern keeper related the history of this building in detail, as told to him by the previous owner. Apparently, 300 to 400 years ago, it had served as a prison holding-area for the condemned of Tyburn Village, then a sub-urb outside London. Before being led through an under-ground tunnel to the executioner's gallows directly across the street, prisoners spent the night in this room.

As he shined the beam of the flashlight to illuminate the imbedded bolts where the manacles had been secured to the wall, Shirl and I were both overwhelmed with feel-ings of confusion, anger, fear, despair and anguish—feel-ings that might be experienced by someone awaiting ex-ecution. Because the energy was so depressing, we did not hang around long enough to physically see any ghosts. However, one could not mistake the condemned spirit's trauma, which remained to this day.

Our castle guide listened to our story with interest as we completed our descent down the stone staircase and entered the huge dining hall on the castle's lower level. He motioned Shirl and me to a far corner of the room. To my surprise, he requested a more detailed description of the aberration I had encountered earlier in the evening.

I reported that I did not "see" a ghost in the literal sense of the word but, instead, sensed it with my mind's eye, like the process of visualizing someone in your imagination. I told him that I really could not provide a physical depic-tion of the phantom energy, other than to say it seemed young, perhaps a boy in his teens. It was not the older man he had alluded to during his tour.

Holding one finger in the air as if to put me on hold, he turned to the remainder of his guests and invited them to help themselves to the refreshments laid out on the stately, antique wooden table in the center of the room.

He motioned us to follow him. Through a labyrinth of passageways, he returned to the bedroom where I had felt the unknown presence. The corridors appeared more ee-rie now, and the few torches that were still burning cast unearthly shadows on the uneven stone walls.

As we entered the ancient bedchamber, our host eagerly confirmed that *this* was the room where other "sensitives" had felt the ghostly presence most often. They, too, saw the spirit of a young boy. He explained that he often described the ghost to visitors as an older man residing in the upper portion of the castle in order to validate true sightings.

He asked about my willingness to initiate contact with this wayward spirit so that he might learn what held him to the castle. Although he had not seen the boy, he was convinced that something unnatural was causing the numerous disturbances emanating from this specific room.

I was on the spot now, about to be tested in a realm I knew little about. At the same time, I was excited to have had my sighting validated, and I responded that I would do the best I could.

Centering myself, I took several deep breaths and opened myself to read this energy. After a few moments I sensed something moving along the far wall, darting back and forth from one corner of the room to another. It initially appeared more like a wisp of fog than an actual human form. I did not visually *see* anything; rather, I *sensed* a form, the way we sense that someone is standing behind us or that something unusual is about to occur, sensations that are unexplainable within the accepted confines of logic.

I projected myself into the center of this energy while describing aloud what I was experiencing. I confronted the unmistakable feelings of a restless young boy, who was extremely angry and confused.

Anger and confusion—two of the same negative feelings I had encountered while in the "murder room" of the mansion at the party with Gerri! They were also among the negative feelings encountered in the basement of the

English pub.

I found myself voicing the young boy's story, much as I channeled during my psychic readings. The tale involved a 12- to 15-year-old lad who had been poisoned in his bed by rival relatives. He was the illegitimate son of the monarch who then owned this castle and much of the surrounding land. He had been killed to prevent his inheriting the kingdom.

The ghost was genuinely angry, and the communication was distorted and confusing. However, one message was quite clear. What bothered him most was that the bed in this room was *not* his. He wanted his own bed back!

During the excursion through the castle, our escort had repeatedly affirmed that nearly all the furniture was authentic to this castle and carefully placed in original locations. But our young friend did not agree! He continued to repeat that he could not be at peace until he could lie in his own bed.

And then I lost my concentration and contact... and he was gone.

Months later, after returning home, I received a letter from our castle host who wanted me to know that my reading had been substantiated. His staff had reviewed the ancient records and had located what they believed was the boy's original bed, one that matched the description the boy had related to me. In addition, the castle's prior keeper had corroborated the fact that the bed in the boy's room was *not* part of the original furnishings as previously stated. The letter concluded that the uneasy negative presence in the room had completely disappeared once the correct bed was returned.

Had I known more at the time, I might have instructed the deceased soul to advance to the "light." Those who work with ghostly essences say these confused, discarnate spirits often are unaware that they have died or remain connected to the earth plane because they died violently. Psychic "ghostbusters" who work with spirits endeavor to convince these misdirected energies that they are no longer served by their connection to the physical realm, that they must go on toward the light.

Most psychics who work with energy will confirm that they personally believe in ghosts. They contend that as the body dies, the spirit generally vacates the vehicle it has inhabited and is drawn to the light. This concept has been documented in several popular books written by well-known and respected medical researchers. One such book, *Life After Life* by Dr. Raymond Moody, contains reports on hundreds of case studies of people who have "died" and then returned to their physical bodies. They tell of going through a tunnel and experiencing the light prior to meeting a respected, spiritual figure. Perhaps that's where the expression "the light at the end of the tunnel" originated?

However, for those who have died and *not* returned to life, it is thought that a portion of their consciousness remains in the physical realm for as long as three months to several years. This essence often seeks connection with a loved one during the grieving period while both adapt to the separation. (Recent popular movies, such as *Ghost* and *Always,* have portrayed this theme.)

Although a fragment of consciousness may remain earthbound after death, the larger essence of the soul-awareness migrates to the light. This dual consciousness of the spiritual self is much like our daydreaming about a pleasant experience while giving our principal attention to some immediate need, such as piloting an automobile through heavy traffic.

Ghosts are considered to be the physical essences of the soul energy that remain behind and love or "haunt" the connection they have with the earth plane. It was this *negative* aspect of consciousness that I had encountered in the murder room of the mansion, the pub basement and the castle bedroom.

When visiting former battlefields, sensitives are often aware of restless energies of young soldiers who have died violent deaths. During World War II, U.S. General George Patton wrote about his perceiving the collective spirits of deceased soldiers at ancient European battle sites. Some claim that the General gained insight from these phantoms, using information from them to plot his successful campaigns during the Allied liberation of Europe.

Ghosts, then, are simply detained or lost souls who have not moved on to the spiritual light because of their binding connections with physical form. Although they seldom have the power to harm anyone physically, they certainly have the ability to capture your attention...

Shirl's father certainly did... three months after he died!

CHAPTER 16

Ghosts Closer to Home

Shortly before we married, Shirl's dad passed away following a long bout with cancer. He lived in Texas during the latter part of his life, and although I had met him once briefly before our marriage, I never really got to know him.

One night, about three months after he left this dimension, Shirl woke from a sound sleep with the intense feeling that someone was in the room! I knew something was amiss when she shook me awake, her unexpected jolt approaching eight on the Richter scale.

After coming down off the ceiling and back into my body, I was aware of Shirl sitting straight up in bed, peering around in the darkness. I instinctively followed her eyes, but I could not locate anything that might justify her concern.

"What was that?" she asked cautiously.

Not having the vaguest clue about what she referred to, I instinctively began to search for something amiss in the room. Turning on the light to satisfy myself that there was nothing out of place, I probed Shirl for more specific information.

"I'm not sure," she said slowly, "but I know I felt something. I think there is someone in the house," she insisted.

Now, it does not make any difference how macho we males perceive ourselves to be; very few of us wish for our mates to report that someone is in the house at four-something in the morning, because the implied suggestion is that *we* go and find out who it is.

Shirl, predictably, wanted *me* to walk through the house to see if anyone was there. I felt more comfortable with the pronoun *we*.

Agreeing, but rejecting the etiquette which maintains that ladies go first, she pushed me forward, assuring me this was the proper procedure. We advanced cautiously through the house, turning on the lights as we went.

Finding no trace of any intruder, we returned to bed. Wide awake now, Shirl still could not shake the feeling that someone was still in our room!

Shirl had lived in this house since her first marriage, and I had heard creepy stories about unexplainable occurrences taking place over the years in the back bedrooms. I still remember the feeling of uncertainty the first time I entered those rooms. It was as if the resident energy of the house did not take kindly to strangers back there.

One account involved a good friend of Shirl's whose husband had died unexpectedly in a freakish automobile accident. Shirl's friend stayed with her for a time while adjusting to her loss.

Late one night while they were both watching TV, Shirl was unexpectedly confronted with a clear visual image of Dick, the deceased husband, standing directly in the center of the room between the two of them!

Before she could react, he put his finger to his lips,

gesturing Shirl to keep quiet. He then moved to his wife, bent over and lovingly placed a kiss on her forehead. At that moment Shirl's friend reached to her forehead as if to wipe away an imaginary wisp of hair. She then stood up and exhaled a deep sigh, saying she was suddenly very tired and was going to bed.

The image of Dick smiled, nodded as if to say everything would be O.K. and then was gone! The next morning at breakfast, Shirl's friend abruptly informed her that she would be leaving. She affirmed that she was now O.K. and ready to resume her life.

It was as if Dick's presence were pivotal to her letting go of her grief.

Shirl never saw Dick again, nor could she ever find the words to tell her friend what she had witnessed.

So here I was, in a darkened bedroom next to my wife of several months, recalling tales of unexplainable occurrences in her house, all the while confronting a growing sense of an uninvited someone or *something* lurking in the room! I had cleansed the house thoroughly with crystal energy before moving in, and I made a mental note to double the cleansing dosage first thing in the morning!

"Can you smell that?" she asked suddenly.

"Smell what?" I replied, shifting my perceptions to my olfactory sense.

"Ohhh no," she moaned in a disappointed voice that left no doubt that she knew exactly what it was. "It's my father."

"Your father?" I repeated. I knew that her relationship with him had been very traumatic over the years and that they had attempted to resolve troubling issues prior to his passing from this physical existence.

"Yes, no question about it," she responded, explaining how she associated the scent with him from when she was a child.

Although I cannot say I could smell anything specific, there was definitely something unsettling in the room. It wasn't physically threatening, but the possible presence of a ghost in the vicinity is, shall we say, unnerving.

Since its intensity remained undiminished and powerful, I felt compelled to try to communicate directly with whatever it was. Although uncertain as to what might occur, I was confident that my guides would support the endeavor and protect me from any harm.

As if intention were the catalyst that could open communication between us, the essence moved directly overhead, as if acknowledging the contact between us. I began to empathize with it on an emotional level in an effort to understand its purpose. I sensed that my personal identity was moving aside as if something else wished to share my space.

Involuntarily I spoke, but the words did *not* originate from me. Instead, they seemed to emanate from a separate source. In the emerging dialogue, full sentences were spoken with a Texas accent, and Shirl recognized phrases and specific mannerisms used by her father when she was a little girl.

It was as though I were a separate witness to a conversation that came tumbling out of my own mouth. It was like reciting the words to a familiar song that took no thought to vocalize.

Shirl's deceased father was *talking through me!*

His essence directly revealed that he was O.K. He had come to settle things with Shirl that had not been resolved during his lifetime. He spoke through me for about 10 minutes or so, and then he departed as suddenly as he had appeared.

His last words were "I love you and I only hope that you can forgive me!"

There is absolutely no question in either of our minds that we encountered the departed spirit of Shirl's father! He discussed situations and personal matters of which I had no knowledge. Perhaps the greatest validation of all is that we *know* what we experienced, and no one can convince us otherwise!

I cannot count the number of people who, upon learning that I am a psychic, will quietly recount an experience of a personal paranormal communication with an entity from the "other side." It is much more common than most people realize.

As mentioned before, ghosts are spirit forms who remain on the earth plane because they retain a strong connection to physical form. Examples include spirits who withdraw from their physical bodies while addicted to drugs or alcohol, mothers who leave a dependent child, and murder victims who seek revenge. Such spirits are often reluctant to completely disconnect from physical existence.

These energies are also summoned, albeit unintentionally, when one plays with a Ouija board, dabbles with automatic writing or stages a seance. They communicate with anyone who will listen, even claiming to be Ben Franklin or your Uncle Harry in order to get attention. Since they are able to access information from the spiritual record depository, they often convince people that they are the specific, deceased individual someone is seeking.

Because these energies will do almost anything to establish and maintain contact with the physical plane, caution must always be used when summoning them. Unless people really know what they are doing, these random energies should not be encouraged. They can mislead, and they are capable of binding themselves to anyone who accepts them. This attachment can often be the forerunner to "possession" or "obsession." If you have doubts about this being possible, consider that the normally conservative Catholic Church performs exorcism ceremonies!

With that being said, recognize that spiritual communication can be harmless if the incorporeal energy initiates the contact and you recognize it as a close friend or relative. The danger lies in purposefully pursuing a deceased spirit to enhance your ego or to delay a spirit's journey into higher consciousness because of your excessive grief or emotional requirements.

Non-physical communication quite often occurs in the form of a dream or intuition rather than in the physical sighting of a ghostly figure. Rest assured; you can discern whether ghosts are friendly or not. A loved one projects only comforting thoughts or loving sensations of peacefulness. A mischievous energy will attempt to solicit a reaction. An evil force has even been known to induce the person contacted into spiritual immorality.

If you have any doubt about a ghost's intention or your own safety, protect yourself first. Just imagine yourself surrounded by the white healing light of God, by Christ Consciousness or by any other sacred image.

Remember the classic Hollywood movies that portray the wise, old priest holding up a crucifix against evil? He is calling the protective energy of God into increased physical consciousness. One law of spiritual physics states that weaker, evil energy cannot break through this more powerful, loving God-energy, which is always accessible. After all, doesn't the *Bible* teach us that we are created in God's image?

It is important to understand that calling on your spiritual guides or angels is immensely different than contacting ghosts. Guides are spiritual energies that originate from a higher, ethereal plane. They are here to assist us, whereas ghosts are often confused souls lacking a physical body. When you request your guides' assistance, you can be assured that they will not lead you astray. Their presence will not frighten you since their energy is "melded" to yours, and they are completely committed to supporting your spiritual growth.

When in doubt as to whether you are encountering a ghost or a guide, wrap yourself in pure white light radiated from your heart chakra. This is your spiritual protection. This is accessing God's power.

Another metaphysical rule of thumb says that if the spirit of good (God) is present and you are a good or light spirit, you will recognize the resultant harmony. If, on the other hand, the energy attracted to you is a dark spirit and you are a good or light spirit, you will feel troubled by its presence.

The reasoning behind this statement is that dissimilar spirits cause discord. When light and dark get together, the result is neither pure light (good) nor dark (absence of good), but gray (confusion and disharmony).

The key to working with these discarnate souls is *intention*. If you are contacted by a loving soul who has left the physical plane, then look to your feelings for confirmation, surround yourself with spiritual white light and make your goal clear.

You do not want to open Pandora's box...

particularly if you don't know what's in the box...

and especially if you've never met Pandora!

CHAPTER 17

Understanding the Past

Following my success with psychic readings, I began slowly to wean myself from Gerri Patton, my psychic mentor. I had rapidly fulfilled my contract with Gerri and completed the 100 readings necessary to become a "bona fide psychic" (whatever that was).

These individual readings led me to unusual people and into strange situations... or was it strange people and unusual situations? I shouldn't have been too surprised at this since I often began conversations in those early days with, "Excuse me, but may I give you a reading?" Not surprisingly, that question led to some interesting encounters, but the readings themselves provided the validation and confidence I needed to venture out on my own.

As I continued to audit classes and attend lectures and workshops, I began to understand the larger spiritual picture and my small role as a karmic player. I became aware that my experiences were not as uncommon as I had first imagined and that being "psychic" or "aware" was *not* unique to this current "New Age." In fact, it became apparent that our species had actually *lost* psychic or intuitive ability as our technology "advanced."

Many anthropologists and historians believe that humankind once used our inherent metaphysical capabilities to a much larger degree than we do today. The early cave dweller had to rely on his or her intuitive senses just to survive! We've just forgotten how because of our increased reliance and dependence on modern science.

So, let's take a small step back in time and explore how past cultures utilized their intuitive, natural ways of "knowing"—the science of *their* day. Perhaps we can relearn what we collectively may have forgotten along the way.

In the era of George Washington and Ben Franklin or, even further back, in the days of Galileo, Bacon and Newton, science walked hand in hand with what are known as the "mystery schools." These schools were, simply stated, the protectors of the great truths of nature and the abstract principles of natural law secretly passed down throughout early history. Many early scientific and philosophical teachers came from the ranks of the Rosicrucians or Masons or belonged to groups who followed Pythagorean, Hermetic or Platonic thought. Whatever their origin, they collectively were the self-appointed keepers of the metaphysical "truth" of their day, insuring that this knowledge did not fall into the wrong hands and that it was not misused.

The two schools of thought—scientific and metaphysical—were intertwined. For example, the Royal Society, formed in the year 1660, was a prestigious, European, scientific think tank. It was the primary influence in the evolution of the physical sciences for hundreds of years. For the first three decades of its existence, the Royal Society was indistinguishable from other ancient secret societies, such as the Rosicrucians and Freemasons. For example, Sir Isaac Newton, president of the Society from 1707 until 1727, was heavily influenced by Hermetic philosophy. When Ben Franklin was inducted in 1756, the Royal Society was still strongly oriented toward the secret, mystical principles of Freemasonry.

As a matter of fact, much of the early symbolism of the United States, formed by such progressive thinkers as Franklin, Washington and Jefferson, was based on a few basic principles of Freemasonry, which were extensions of ancient esoteric and spiritual teachings. (Examine the rear side of a U.S. dollar bill and you will view several examples of Masonry symbolism.)

Robert Macoy, in his *General History of Freemasonry*, pays a magnificent tribute to the part played by the ancient mystery schools in the advancement of modern human culture. He writes, "It appears that all the perfection of civilization and all the advancement made in philosophy, science and art among the ancients are due to those institutions which, under the veil of the mystery schools, sought to illustrate the sublime truths of religion, morality and virtue."

Present day skeptics delight in associating some of these ancient belief systems with the practice of alchemy and sorcery, which are today considered evil or, at best, superstitious and false.

No wonder! With the decline of virtue, which has preceded the destruction of every major nation in history, the truth of the "Mysteries" has become perverted. In alchemy, for example, the pursuit of natural metaphysical knowledge was bypassed, through greed, in favor of changing iron into gold. Sorcery replaced divine magic. Even crystal energy and pyramid power became the misunderstood tools of the imitators of Pythagoras, who taught the pure use of the natural mathematical forces of the universe over 2,500 years ago!

The few who worked with these pure metaphysical concepts *in the manner in which they were intended,* however, demonstrated success beyond belief.

What was kept hidden by the mystery schools—the self-proclaimed protectors of "the truth"—was handed down each generation to an elite few and is now beginning to be openly practiced by some modern-day medicine men or shamans of native cultures. And these same truths are being slowly released into our current culture by way of the New Age or planetary consciousness.

However, resistance to these ancient truths is not unique to the 20th century. Some historical leaders embraced principles that most men of their day rejected as "primitive" and, therefore, invalid. Both Plato and Michelangelo, for example, were said to be initiates of secret, sacred orders and were often severely criticized for holding outmoded, superstitious concepts. Few lauded them as "knowledgeable" when they began to make public a few of the secret, philosophic principles of the mystery schools.

Were these simply the false beliefs of rudimentary and uneducated people who grasped at straws because they lacked sophistication? After all, now that we are approaching the 21st century, with modern science having disproved the ignorance of old, *we* are far too advanced and knowledgeable for such primitive thinking. Certainly there cannot be any basis of fact in these old superstitions and belief systems.

Or can there?

Let's take a peek back into history...

In ancient societies, the tribal elders would always consult with the tribal shaman before making important decisions affecting the well-being of the village. It was the shaman's job to seek council with the native spirits and enlist their support to insure a positive outcome.

Superstition? Maybe, but the late Dr. Joseph Campbell, the world-renowned authority on mythology, claims that belief systems develop through a succession of correct interpretations of factual happenings. Shamans would have had to maintain a successful track record to have continuously held their authority.

Early Scandinavian leaders consulted the *runes* for their insight. The runes consist of 24 individual tiles plus one blank (although the English sometimes used as many as 33), each imprinted with a letter of an ancient alphabetic script that possesses a meaningful name and sound. Runes, whose origins date back at least 3,000 years, were widely used in Iceland as well as in Northern and Western Europe in the late Middle Ages for obtaining answers to a question or problem. Any number of runes were drawn or thrown, depending on the complexity of the answer sought. Each rune had a separate meaning, and it was the purview of the shaman to interpret the results.

To illustrate the influence of the runes, we note that when the Anglo-Saxon high chieftains would meet in a conclave, they referred to their secret deliberations as a rune. When Bishop Wulfila made his translation of the *Bible* into fourth century Gothic, he employed the word "rune" for mystery.

Would the runes continue to be consulted if they didn't work?

In a like manner, the *I Ching* (pronounced "E Ching") may be the oldest book on the planet. Called the Book of Changes, it has been written about by notables from Confucius to Carl Jung. This ancient oracle, like the runes, remains widely consulted by people even today.

Fu Hsi, the legendary ruler of China during the third

millennium B.C., is said to have originally discovered the arrangements of eight trigrams forming the 64 hexagrams of the *I Ching* on the shell of a tortoise. Today, hexagrams are created when the person who seeks an answer to a specific question throws three coins six times; the pattern of "heads and tails" appearing determines a resultant hexagram, along with a second if the situation is in transition. The first hexagram provides insight into the current circumstance of a questionable situation, and the second suggests a resolution or change in the near future.

Since it survived this length of time and is still in use, the *I Ching* must have value.

How about the mastery of the forces of nature? According to an ever-increasing number of believers, the pyramids of the ancient Egyptian era were constructed through control of some currently unknown natural force, such as crystal power or levitation. Only such theories might explain the laser precision of pyramid construction that *cannot* be duplicated today, even with the use of modern construction techniques. Certainly slaves, even in countless numbers, could not have pushed and lifted these multi-ton stone blocks into place with the exacting tolerances found in these structures.

Could extraterrestrials have assisted?

There are many cultures and societies existing today whose traditions and legends suggest that our planet has been visited by universal light- and time-travelers for some time. Consider some currently unexplainable phenomena, such as mysterious abductions, cryptic crop circles, cattle mutilations and the like.

Additionally, several well-respected authors argue that many prehistoric cave paintings contain figures resembling space beings and drawings of flying machines. In several of its chapters, the *Old Testament* refers to "flying chariots" descending from the skies. A UFO in the language of the day?

In the face of such testimonies and mysteries, how can we state unequivocally that forces of which we are not currently familiar do not exist?

It is thought by some that the current medicine men or shamans of the African and Native American cultures are still able to communicate directly with these natural energy forces. I know personally a television reporter who, while working for CBS News during the days of Walter Cronkite, witnessed this process firsthand.

My friend had been given the assignment of interviewing a certain African shaman. Upon arriving at the shaman's remote village after a long and arduous journey, my friend was informed by one of the tribal elders that their shaman had left the village with a hunting party. None of the villagers knew when he would return.

After convincing the tribal leader that the shaman be informed of his arrival, my friend watched the elder walk to one of the largest and oldest trees at the edge of the encampment and begin speaking to it. He asked that the tree pass word of the shaman's visitor to the other trees of the forest.

The elder then sat at the base of the tree and waited.

Sometime later, the elder stood up, placed his ear to the tree and listened. He then returned and disclosed to my friend that the shaman would arrive back at the village during the evening of the full moon, three days hence. He added that their hunt had gone well.

Exactly three days later (as the full moon rose in the evening sky) the shaman appeared, fully aware that there was a visitor awaiting his return. He also confirmed that the hunt had been very successful. When queried about how he knew that someone wished to see him, the shaman simply said, "The trees told me!"

Having had extensive contact with both Native American, African and Brazilian shamans, I am convinced that many of them are authentic. They are successful in their practice because they totally believe in themselves and what they do. Whether they speak to spirit guides, visit the upper or lower worlds in an altered state of consciousness, converse with the trees or commune with spaceships, they are unmistakably able to benefit those they are serving.

Several points about shamans are noteworthy.

There is usually only one shaman per tribe or clan and an apprentice in training. The understudy is generally the son of the shaman but may be selected from another family as the result of a trance, vision or dream of the current officeholder.

The shaman generally is male. He does not eat meat, smoke tobacco or drink alcohol. He receives his "knowing" from varying sources, although it is typically from a vision or dream and almost always in an altered state of consciousness, occasionally drug-induced by way of a spiritual ceremony.

The shaman never charges for his services, although he will accept food or lodging for his work. He never exploits the information for selfish purposes but, instead, uses it for the greater good.

He always credits the source of the information as originating from God or a religious or moral equivalent.

And anyone who publicly calls himself a shaman usually isn't!

CHAPTER 18

Psychic Surgery

There are many who will attest to the power of a shaman!

As mentioned in the previous chapter, a shaman is, essentially, a native priest or medicine man who communes with spirits, be they natural earth energies or unseen cosmic forces. Stated another way, he is a psychic or parapsychologist working with the tools of his trade.

In order to understand the workings of a shaman practitioner in left brain, logical terms, let's begin by briefly examining our Western scientific theories regarding the nature of things.

Early Newtonian physics basically stated that all observable events of the universe were predictable once they were understood. This concept was in vogue for hundreds of years until quantum physicians happened along and suggested, among other things, that the very act of observation changes the reality of the object or event observed.

"Fundamentally, the observer creates reality by observing it," asserted Niels Bohr and Albert Einstein in their *Copenhagen Interpretation*, the mainstay of today's understanding of physics.

The scientifically "primitive" shaman, on the other hand, adds a slightly different twist. He believes it is not the *act* of observation but *how* something is observed that dictates the reality we perceive. "Change the how of it and you change the what of it," states Fred Wolf, a quantum physicist, in his book *The Eagle's Quest*.

The shaman believes that we each see the reality we *intend* to see, with intention being the key. The shaman merely extends his intention to the object in order to alter it. In doing this, he creates the desired result.

Where Newton might say, "Seeing is believing," quantum physicists would state, "You get what you expect!" In shaman physics, the practitioner might summarize it this way: "Intention creates perception, and perception determines reality!"

Most Native American shamans equate God to the Ultimate Dreamer. The shaman consciously expands his experience in order to *enter* the world of God's dream and *become* a part of the dream. By this method, the shaman frees himself from the limited, fixed pattern of perception we have been taught, enters an alternate form of reality and interacts with it.

Shamans may practice their craft for "good" by healing on an individual or planetary plane, but it can be practiced for "evil" by casting spells or creating negativity to control others or enhance their own personal power.

Shamans continue to ply their trade today, particularly in remote, primitive locations in third world countries. However, they can also be found in more modern areas—in Native American tribes, for example, or in Siberia, the

Caribbean Islands and Central and South America.

Since shamans are the psychics of their culture, Shirl and I very much wanted to meet them in their domain. Of course we realized that authentic shamans are difficult to locate, and we would not find them listed on the standard Gray Line tour brochures! So, as a first step on this seemingly improbable quest for contact, we began to manifest the concept that either we would be led to shamans or that they would find us.

We did not have to wait long...

We were provided a unique opportunity to accompany Dr. Stanley Krippner—a psychologist, author and internationally known authority on shaman practices—on one of his expeditions to visit shaman healers in Brazil. There we had the privilege of meeting authentic shamans and partaking in some of their authentic rituals, spiritual healings, exorcisms and psychic surgeries. Each shaman claimed differing sources for his power—from the Great Spirit to communication with UFOs to Amazon nature spirits.

One such Brazilian, whom we had the exceptional opportunity to spend time with, is a man named Mauricio, known in his country by the single name, just as Cher or Elvis are known in ours. Mauricio is a medically uneducated psychic who, although well-known for his ability to heal, is *not* listed in *Who's Who of the American Medical Association*, at least not in their current edition. He is unique because he *channels* a famous Brazilian physician who died a physical death nearly a century ago!

We were driven to a clandestine location in the city of São Paulo, Brazil, and informed that we would have the honor of observing this famous psychic surgeon firsthand! We learned that he would conduct his psychic surgery in a "safe house" because such surgery is considered illegal in Brazil. We were told that one of the reasons it is prohibited is because Brazilian healers practicing psychic surgical procedures threaten the economy of the professional medical community. Although healers have been doing this work for centuries, they have been recently forced underground and can only practice in secret. Nevertheless, they serve the vast majority of the people who cannot afford the high cost of modern medicine.

Upon our arrival, we were welcomed into an incredibly beautiful home located in one of the very few wealthy areas of this generally poor country. We were escorted through the length of this opulent dwelling to a smaller building, which normally served as a dressing room for the swimming pool.

When Mauricio arrived, he entered the room and began shaking hands with the dozen or so invited guests, much like a politician at a fund-raising event. He was a gentle man, full of self-assurance, yet surprisingly shy and introverted.

As two women in starched white uniforms laid out modern and frightening surgical instruments, Mauricio slowly explained through our interpreter that he would attain the altered state of a trance, then step aside, allowing the spirit of a deceased German doctor by the name of Dr. Fritz to assume control of his body. Mauricio revealed that he had no formal Western medical training, and it would be Dr. Fritz who would diagnose and operate on the non-anesthetized patients through the instrument of Mauricio's body.

He completed his orientation by naming several other doctors who channeled through him from time to time, but reiterated that he expected Dr. Fritz to appear on this day. (We later learned that he was not the only psychic who channeled Dr. Fritz. Ever since his death nearly 100 years ago, Dr. Fritz has worked through several mediums at any one time, as Seth or Michael energies do in the United States.)

The soft-spoken Mauricio then smiled at us, graciously bowed and quietly exited the room.

A few moments later, what appeared to be an entirely *different* man reentered the room and introduced himself in a loud and obnoxious voice as the "world famous Dr. Fritz." Waving his arms wildly in the air to accentuate his opening remarks, he spoke to us in rapid Portuguese, which our own interpreter loosely translated into English. Dr. Fritz took a full five minutes to inform us, in essence, that he was rarin' to go.

Mauricio's personality and appearance had changed considerably! He was no longer the rather shy, middle-aged man we had met earlier. Instead, his eyes bulged wildly, reminding me of a bug-eyed, mysterious Peter Lorre in the classic movie *The Maltese Falcon.* He paced nervously, as though feeding off the shocked looks of his captive audience. It struck me that he would be the *last* person I would want near me with a scalpel in his hand!

Without wasting anymore time, Dr. Fritz selected a half dozen dart-like objects and flicked them one at a time into the chest of his first patient, whom the nurses had just positioned on the operating table. Our English-speaking interpreter informed us that the man had come seeking treatment for hypertension.

After a few moments, Dr. Fritz removed the needles and, with a twisting motion of his head, instructed his assistants to reposition the man onto his stomach. Grabbing a scalpel from a tray of sharp medical tools, the "doctor" made a vertical, four-inch incision alongside the man's backbone, beginning between his shoulder blades. He then inserted a set of long forceps fully eight inches into this slit and set it into final position with several heavy blows from the heel of his hand.

This entire procedure probably took less than one minute.

Dr. Fritz, speaking to us more rapidly than the interpreter could translate, paced back and forth while explaining how the forceps were doing the required healing without his moving them. After elaborating in detail, as if taking great delight in presenting his technique to queasy first-year medical students, the doctor unexpectedly walked over to *me*, one of more than a dozen people in the room, and smiled. "Withdraw the instrument," he commanded in no uncertain terms while looking directly into my eyes.

Fearing that if I did, I would lose my lunch all over the table and probably lose his patient as well, I respectfully declined, shaking my head no, audible sounds failing me as I tried to form words with my mouth.

"Chuck, he is instructing you to withdraw his forceps," I heard a loud, excited voice say on my immediate left. Dr. Stanley Krippner, the parapsychologist who had arranged the trip and testified to the credibility of this Brazilian shaman, had slipped in beside me and was nudging me forward.

I turned and looked at Dr. Krippner with totally disbelieving eyes, feet frozen to the floor of the makeshift operating theater. "It is a great honor to be selected," he explained. "In fact," he added, "I have rarely seen any psychic surgeon select an observer to assist. You *can't* say no!"

Standing directly in front of me with an amused expression on his face, Dr. Fritz repeated his command, his eyes dancing with power. "I have selected a North American healer to assist me," he reported to the assembled group, all of whom were relieved that he had not selected them and were now awaiting my response.

The mere sight of blood makes me squeamish, but, feeling the pressure from Dr. Krippner, the support from the other observers and, more specifically, the unmistakable directive from the wild-eyed surgeon waving a sharp instrument in front of my face, I found myself walking forward. (I say "found myself walking forward" because the *real* me would *never* have done that! It was as if some higher source of energy were pressing the buttons and pulling the levers, and I was strictly a passive observer of myself in action.)

Slowly, I walked to the table, tentatively grabbed the small amount of metal which was left protruding from the man's back and pulled.

The instrument would not budge.

I grabbed it more deliberately with two hands and pulled again.

It didn't move!

Not until I grasped it firmly with a cloth lying nearby and really tugged did the forceps begin to disengage from deep in the patient's back... along with an appropriate amount of blood and ooze.

Dr. Fritz, not missing a beat, placed some salve on the wound and applied several butterfly bandages and a few quick sutures for good measure. Totally pleased with himself, his eyes bulging more than ever, he then announced that he had successfully corrected the patient's problem.

The room was filled with nervous silence.

With assistance from the two nurses, the patient slowly lifted himself to a sitting position and, to everyone's complete astonishment, asked when the operation would take place. He looked surprised and relieved when told that it already had and that his hypertension would no longer be a factor. After embracing Dr. Fritz, he exited the room without assistance, almost as if nothing out of the ordinary had occurred.

No one else complained of hypertension for the remainder of the day!

While in the company of the amazing Dr. Fritz, we observed him complete seven other procedures, some of which were as dramatic as the one described above. All of his treatments began by his flicking long needles into various parts of the patient's body and allowing them to set for several moments before removing them.

In every case, the effectiveness of the cure seemed roughly proportional to the level of belief each patient exhibited in the doctor and his procedure. In one case, Dr. Fritz inserted tweezers up into a woman's nose for the treatment of a sinus condition. She appeared less than enthusiastic when he explained what he was about to do and, as a result, resisted the procedure. The treatment turned out to be unsuccessful with the outcome being severe pain and an ugly bruise around her eye.

However, in another instance, a dart was placed *in* the eye of a woman who had complained of vision problems. This patient barely flinched at its insertion and maintained calm while on the operating table. She walked away under her own power at the conclusion of the procedure, exclaiming to anyone who would listen that her vision had improved immensely.

While Dr. Fritz was performing these procedures, a recognized and respected English journalist standing next to me said that she had seen him accomplish his healing work dozens of times over the years. She assured me that the patients had neither been hypnotized nor been given drugs prior to surgery.

"They simply believe in him," she stated.

Between patients, she related stories about other psychic surgeries she had witnessed him perform. She reported that he frequently extracted gooey substances from his patients' bodies, *without cutting the skin,* while observers surrounded the operating table, practically eliminating the opportunity for trickery or sleight of hand.

"Who's next?" Dr. Fritz asked the group of spectators when he had exhausted his supply of patients.

My wife, half kiddingly, asked me if I wanted exploratory surgery on my lower intestinal tract or an operation to silence the incessant ringing in my ears. I told her thanks for asking, but I had already done my part.

Much to everyone's amazement, a Canadian woman who was one of our traveling companions calmly climbed onto the table and laid down on her back. Without communicating, Dr. Fritz gave her a quick glance and, selecting a half dozen new darts, flicked them into her lower abdomen. After pausing several moments, he slowly withdrew them and announced with a great flourish that he had just cured a persistent infection in her kidney.

Our friend lifted herself from the table, thanked him with a shy smile and confirmed to the group that she *did* have an infection in her kidney. The only other person in the room who had known of her condition was her husband, and he had not said a word about it to anyone.

Of the eight people we observed being treated that day, the only two who appeared to have experienced pain were the ones who seemed to have the least amount of faith in the doctor and his techniques. The six who fully believed and trusted in him exhibited no pain and appeared to have benefitted the most from the healing.

As we departed the room, we were all truly amazed at what we had seen! You couldn't help but believe!

CHAPTER 19

Shamans and Orishas

We met a number of shaman psychic healers and surgeons while in Brazil, each employing one or more of four basic healing techniques. They claim either to tap into the energy of one of 12 major spiritual forms called *orishas*, be guided by earth nature spirits, channel deceased healers or surgeons or take instruction from light beings originating from beyond our solar system or dimension. Although these shamans employ varying tools or methods, many repeatedly experience positive results and have numerous loyal followers who travel great distances to be healed.

These Brazilian practitioners concur that *most* physical illnesses are caused by either a person's faulty belief system or by negative spirits which have invaded or attached themselves to an individual's energy field. In either case, they believe that many "dis - eases" that cause the physical body to malfunction are the result of a spiritual malady.

Although some healers resort to psychic surgery, most

claim that they cure their patient by altering or cleaning their spiritual essence. In some cases, they prescribe a ritual to be followed or a natural herb to be ingested.

We were extremely fortunate to observe and work with another shaman healer—a surgeon/spiritual healer who employs all of the techniques mentioned. Antonio DePadua is a priest in one of the Universal Spiritist Churches. Like other holistic practitioners throughout the world, he believes that our illnesses are essentially spiritual in nature, and he cleanses, prescribes and sometimes operates on the spiritual or ethereal body to heal the physical one. We were told DePadua conducted as many ceremonies as were required to heal all who sought his assistance, neither requesting nor accepting money for his healing work.

Shirl and I had the rare honor to experience DePadua's healing technique personally!

We first observed the cleansing, deobsessing and depossessing of offending spirits. In a religious ritual performed one evening in DePadua's temple, about 20 of his flock entered a light trance state aided by the hypnotic rhythm of pounding drums. As we stood alongside them, these followers assumed the roles of mediums by accepting the energies of individual spirits or orishas—becoming mediums for them.

These orishas are not personal spirit guides, but communal energy forms which can inhabit a medium's body. All three of the largest spiritist groups or sects we observed in Brazil summoned these energy forms during a religious ceremonial procedure for the sole purpose of healing. The orishas are 12 in number and are similar in character, interestingly enough, to the 12 astrological signs of the zodiac. Each person serving as a medium may have access to one or more orisha.

As DePadua's followers began to move and dance to

the cadence of three drummers, their facial expressions and body energy changed at the *precise moment* each medium received his or her summoned spirit forms. We watched the auras of the dancers become larger and more vibrant against the whitewashed walls as the tempo and volume of drumming increased.

In Brazil there are approximately equal numbers of male and female mediums, with the chief priest being the male leader of the group, and this was true on this night. As each medium yielded to the powerful transforming energy, he or she exhibited one of three general personality types.

About a third of the disciples accepted various orishas who appeared to transform the consenting mediums into "old black men"—they hunched over as if they had aged in the space of a few minutes. Others took on the essence of "Indians," scowling authentically, many dancing in wild circular movements like whirling dervishes. Orishas converted the remaining group into "young children," who were playful, giggling and childlike in their mannerisms.

Then the cadence of the drumming slowed. Antonio DePadua, who had all the while been motionless, praying before a large statue of Jesus, slowly turned and faced his congregation. In a trance state himself, his eyes were narrow and incredibly peaceful. He was no longer the personable priest to whom we had spoken at length prior to the ceremony, but an enlightened spiritual master.

For the next five to six hours, he and his parishioners conducted "passes" or "aura cleansings" on each of about 200 to 300 people who had come to be healed. Such "passes" were intended to neutralize negative forces that had attached themselves to these people.

These simple village folk, many of whom had traveled hours, were first ushered through two lines of DePadua's trancing mediums, who cleansed their auras. When they eventually reached DePadua, he summoned an appropriate spirit. If necessary, he performed an exorcism on a patient who he determined was possessed or obsessed by an uninvited parasite or "demon" energy whose goal was to control the host body entirely—possession—or to alter and influence the host body's natural, healthy energy flow—obsession. DePadua removed the offending spirit by placing his hands on the one possessed or obsessed and commanding the spirit to leave. He physically extracted this negative force with his hands, immediately relocating it onto a willing medium who was poised to accept it.

The medium, whose karma it was to assume this task, yelled and thrashed about as he fought this evil force inside his own body. Once the evil energy was defeated, the medium regurgitated it out of his body through his mouth, giving it over to a spiritual, healing light energy which entered the room as the ceremony began. This light absorbed and dispelled the remainder of the offensive spirit, then slowly faded to its previous level in the room.

Several hours into the ceremony, Dr. Krippner, our group leader, was given the rare honor of assisting DePadua. Together, they worked to remove several possessing forces from the faithful. When he touched the heads of those who required exorcism, Dr. Krippner later told our small traveling group, he felt as if he had contacted something slimy or muddy. As he and DePadua collectively transferred this energy to a nearby medium assigned to receive it, he actually saw sparks at the point of contact. He confided that after completing each healing, he felt relieved of a heavy burden. Dr. Krippner concluded that he had no doubts regarding the authenticity of the process.

Each person traveling with Dr. Krippner was given the opportunity to experience a cleansing and healing from

DePadua as well as from other shamans we met on our journey. Though none of the shamans had any prior information on our group, they *all* spent more time with the same few individuals who most needed the healing!

Once during the ceremony, DePadua asked Dr. Krippner if one woman traveling with us (who, we later found out, had cancer) knew she had a serious illness. He did not want to alarm her if she were unaware of her condition. I witnessed this kind of knowing and compassion from several shamans.

The following day we were invited to both witness and *receive* spiritual-body psychic surgery, the second method of healing Antonio DePadua offered.

A member of his staff met us and ushered us to a secret, remote operating theater located about 45 minutes from the town where we were staying. The facility, covered only by a thatched roof supported on poles attached to a smooth concrete floor, contained two operating tables. It was enclosed in a natural circle of trees, considered a genuine power spot by those who believe in the concept of geomancy.

(Geomancy is an ancient holistic science and philosophy integrating ecology, architecture, sacred geometry, astronomy and other natural sciences. Those who employ geomancy locate positive earth energy and a place of natural healing by considering lay lines of earth energies, biomagnetic energies, labyrinths and megalithic formations. Egyptian and Central American pyramids, ancient stone circles like Stonehenge, ancient cemeteries, places of worship, passage mounds and even European Gothic cathedrals were constructed on sites with positive geomancy qualities.)

It was obvious that this Brazilian medicine man was attuned to these forces of nature!

The life-size statue of Jesus used in the previous evening's temple ritual was in one corner. Along the perimeter of this open-air shelter, a series of tables held surgical instruments similar to those used by the wild-eyed Dr. Fritz, but our Brazilian translator assured us that DePadua would *not* be cutting into our physical bodies, only our ethereal ones.

Her assurance calmed our nervousness only somewhat!

DePadua entered the room and explained, through our interpreter, that he would operate for as long as it took to treat everyone who requested his healing. Looking around, I counted more than 60 people who somehow knew DePadua would be here, and I noticed more still arriving. The scarcity of automobiles in the adjacent parking area suggested that many had made the long trip on foot!

DePadua introduced us to his mother and father, who spoke with us while he began the 20 minute process of receiving the spirit of the German doctor whom he would channel this day. Strains of Mozart, a particular favorite of this deceased surgeon, emanated from a portable, crank-up phonograph sitting near the feet of the large statue of Jesus.

Proudly, displaying sketches of various doctors their son channels, his parents approached our group. His father explained that DePadua insists on examining X-rays or medical test results on every patient before operating on them. His patients, after their psychic surgery, are required to return to their Western-trained doctors for a second set of tests to confirm the results of DePadua's procedures. We were shown documents—prepared by reputable medical sources—which confirmed that DePadua's surgeries had completely corrected the medical condition of *more than one third of his cases*! This is an amazing statistic when you consider that many people who seek DePadua's unorthodox procedures come only as a last resort because their condition has been diagnosed as *untreatable by modern medicine!*

DePadua not only had invited our group to witness this event, but he had graciously agreed to perform surgery on any of us, waiving his usual X-ray stipulation. To my surprise, six people from our group of a dozen volunteered.

To my greater amazement, Shirley and I were two of them!

I was concerned about the lower intestinal disease my "fannyologist" had diagnosed and treated some years before, but had not cured. Shirl wished relief from the ever-present pain in her upper back and neck, particularly troublesome for her when on arduously physical journeys, such as this one.

Because of the sheer numbers of those who had come for surgery, we concluded that if we did not like what we witnessed, we could back out before our names were called. Then the names of the first two patients were announced... and *my* name was one of them.

As I was helped onto one of the two tables in preparation for surgery by someone who, at that very moment, was entering an altered state of consciousness, I seriously questioned the wisdom of my judgment. My left brain screamed, "What the hell do you think you are doing?" while my right brain calmly said, "Trust that everything will be O.K."

My view of what was happening to the patient scheduled before me on the adjacent operating table was partially blocked by nurses preparing me for surgery. All I saw was the expressionless faces of the group of onlookers surrounding him. The quiet was deafening as I stared at the very sharp surgical tools that would, presumably, be used... on *me!*

There was a sudden movement and then *he* was there, standing over me. As he rearranged the sheet that covered my partially naked body, DePadua's face looked incredibly peaceful. When I looked into his partially opened eyes, I was totally captivated by his intensely spiritual and reassuring look.

His calmness resonated throughout my body.

Then he reached for a scalpel, and I immediately began to reevaluate the decision-making process which had left me in this highly exposed position!

I caught the eye of my wife; her expression translated to, "Relax, I'm sure everything will be O.K."

"Yeah, O.K. for her; it isn't *her* groin this Brazilian is waving a knife at," I thought to myself. I shut my eyes, totally relying on the theory that if I can't see it, it will go away!

When DePadua began the procedure, I did not feel anything physically penetrate my skin, yet I was absolutely convinced that something had entered my body. I felt as if DePadua had cut into me; yet *I felt no pain.* The sensation was not unpleasant. It resembled the rumbling feelings my stomach experiences when digesting a heavy meal.

Three or four times I did peek to assure myself that no sharp object protruded from my body.

The operation probably lasted less than 15 minutes. But when someone is standing above you in a glassy-eyed trance with a sharp scalpel in his hand, it seems quite a bit longer. When DePadua finished, he reported that I had colitis (which I knew) but would not have any dangerous recurrence at this time (my own doctor's assessment at a recent examination prior to this trip). This was remarkable to me considering DePadua had been told only that I had a "concern" in the general area of my abdomen.

It was not until the following morning that I noticed the scar where DePadua had made my "incision!"

Shirl, who had several vertebrae fused as the result of an auto accident many years before we were married, had her operation later in the day. Her experience was similar to mine. She was aware of sensations in her neck and back during the procedure but felt nothing on the surface of her body. After the operation and the prayer session, tears in her eyes and a big grin on her face told me that she had regained flexibility and movement in her neck.

Later DePadua paid me a great honor by requesting my assistance in the diagnosis of several patients. Perhaps because of the intensity and pureness of the energy in that space and time, I needed only to open my mouth to hear medical words and phrases—beyond my intellectual knowledge—come tumbling out!

My visit to what some call a backwards, third world country reinforced my belief that our modern society's exclusive reliance on technical advances has its limitations. We assume that if it can't be proven under strict scientific laboratory conditions, it hasn't much value. It's the old belief system—"If you don't see it, it isn't there."

This trip convinced me that our state-of-the-art medical technology is not the only system that works. For example, on the staffs of the most modern Brazilian hospitals, you'll find not only physicians schooled in Western methods, but also nearly as many old-fashioned spiritual healers.

Perhaps the Brazilians have access to a wider range of healing than we do.

Many of us are taught early on to rely entirely on our logical thinking. We are schooled to accept that intuitively based psychic or metaphysical healing has little, if any, value or credibility. In fact, an active, well-known professional organization in the United States boasts that they will award $10,000 to the first so-called psychic who can *prove* a psychic event. They say all they need is one demonstration that meets their criteria.

The fact that they still have their 10 grand illustrates that they will never be convinced. Their reality is that psychic events do not exist, period!

Whether the healings we witnessed on our journey are verifiable scientifically or whether they occurred due to the influence of the mind, who cares? If I am provided with a placebo and my illness is cured, so what? In our experience, the people who underwent psychic surgery believed in their cure, and they *were cured!*

Tell the thousands of Brazilians who swear by their cures that psychic events do not exist.

… And tell that to my wife who, for the first time since her accident, has free movement in her neck!

CHAPTER 20

Mystic Healer

Once on the metaphysical path, the new traveler is often so fascinated with what is "out there" that he or she can become addicted to the search for new experiences, if only to validate previous ones. As a result of our interest, Shirl and I have encountered paranormal events that become unbelievable in the telling; prior to my writing this book, we hesitated to share accounts of such events with others, fearful of damaging our credibility.

People in other parts of the world, however, are *not* as negatively conditioned as Americans—doubters and spurners of what cannot be rationally explained. While traveling in Brazil and other parts of the world, we saw that people consider metaphysical events as rather commonplace.

We Westerners are quick to conclude that because primitive societies are largely uneducated by our standards, they are easily duped into believing in "superstitions." We think that *they* have difficulty separating fiction from reality.

Shirl's and my direct experiences suggest otherwise!

For example, we observed a UFO firsthand, and we have met whole communities of South American people who speak with "aliens" regularly! We have witnessed people levitate! We know a man who dematerializes his arm in front of witnesses, and we know individuals who are able to transport themselves thousands of miles instantaneously!

And we have witnessed a Brazilian healer emit near-blinding flashes of lights from various parts of his body in full view of more than 100 witnesses!

This Brazilian light healer, Mauricio Panisset, came to a four-day, metaphysical retreat in the California desert, led by the well-known actress and metaphysician, Shirley MacLaine, who had met him on one of her earlier metaphysical journeys. She had flown him to California—his first appearance away from his remote village community.

Mauricio (coincidentally having the same first name as the psychic surgeon who channeled Dr. Fritz) was a simple, pleasant-looking man who appeared to be in his early 40s. His clothing and mannerisms suggested that he was a rural farm worker, not the more sophisticated person we had expected. Ms. MacLaine described him as a cross between Charlie Chaplin and Cantinflas, the comic genius who appeared with her in the movie *Around the World in 80 Days.* I couldn't have described him better. He was short, had shocking white hair and was a bit overweight.

When she introduced him, Mauricio stood quietly in the corner of the large room, as if overwhelmed by this large group's interest in him. Since he spoke no English, MacLaine briefly related the story of his miraculous healing technique, beginning with an event from his childhood.

Apparently, while still just a small boy, he saw shimmering balls of lights, which he said would often follow and "talk" to him. He told no one, fearful of being disbelieved or ridiculed. During his adolescence, these experiences with lights repeatedly occurred.

Years later, as a young construction worker, Mauricio fell more than 100 feet while repairing the top of a high tower, but he suffered nothing more than a small fracture. He was convinced that the lights that had spoken to him in his youth protected him. After his fall, the lights appeared more frequently, and, for the first time, they instructed him to use the power they gave him to heal others. Since Mauricio had no conscious knowledge, ability or interest in being a healer, he ignored them. Soon after, he became very ill.

Then one night the lights reappeared. A blue light separated itself from the others and transformed into a light being who called itself Uhr. It instructed Mauricio to heal the sick in his community; only in this way could he cure his own illness. As he began to follow Uhr's specific instructions, his own health improved.

When the lights next approached Mauricio, a bright yellow one materialized into a being calling itself Akron and gave him further instructions on the healing that was to become his life's journey.

As he worked more with this mysterious healing energy force, observers occasionally noticed small flashes of light emanating from Mauricio's fingertips during the healing process.

Then one evening, as he was sitting outside looking up at the night sky, three lights descended from the stars and formed a single ball of light directly in front of Mauricio. A combined energy calling itself Enoch spoke telepathically, instructing him to devote all his time to healing with his newly developed skills.

Shirley MacLaine's audience shifted uncomfortably,

finding it difficult to believe the story she told on the third day of what had been, until then, a totally credible workshop experience.

Suddenly, a flash of light illuminated the entire room.

MacLaine, stopping abruptly in mid-sentence, chastised whoever had broken our agreement barring all cameras from the seminar.

Then there was a second flash, and a third, followed by six or seven bursts of brilliant light in rapid succession.

"Oh my God, look!" shouted a woman jumping to her feet, pointing to Mauricio.

In the corner of the room, awaiting the completion of this introduction, Mauricio twitched uncontrollably, as if in convulsions. Each time his body jerked, light flashed from a different part of his body.

"I was afraid of this," mumbled MacLaine to those of us close enough to hear. Quickly motioning several of her seminar aides to assist Mauricio out of the room, she said that everything was O.K. and urged us to stay where we were. She then turned and exited quickly.

The silence in the room was profound.

Minutes later MacLaine reappeared and calmly informed us that everything was under control. The audience's anticipation was so intense, she explained, that Mauricio, having never before been in front of a group as large as this one, had grown nervous and experienced uncontrollable bursts of energy.

She requested that we close our eyes while she led us through one of her effective, guided meditations in order to lower the anticipatory energy level in the room. When the visualization was completed, she suggested that we each lower our expectations, although I doubt many of us had the slightest clue about what to expect at this point.

After a moment Mauricio reentered and, taking command, walked directly to the raised platform, which served as a stage.

"The energy patterns need to be dispersed," he told MacLaine through his interpreter, "or else my own circuits will be overloaded again."

He then walked throughout the room, waving his arms, forming us into pods of no more than 10 to 12 people. When he was satisfied that we were positioned properly, he returned to the platform. He stated that he would demonstrate his healing *if* the "lights" agreed.

We did not have to wait long.

Ms. MacLaine directed someone to dim the overhead lights so we could see the healing lights clearly. Mauricio raised his hands toward a group MacLaine had seated near the front because each had expressed a critical need for healing. He stepped off the platform and circled them, all the while twitching his arms, as if not knowing exactly how to hold them.

Suddenly, an extremely bright light from the center of Mauricio's chest pierced the dimly lit room. The intensity of the burst was not unlike a camera's flash from several feet away. Some reported seeing a pure flash of white light; others, a blue-white beam extending from Mauricio's chest to the individual being healed.

But *everyone* saw the light!

He walked around this group several times, each time sending a discharge of light to one or more in the group. Each time, the light seemed to emanate from a different part of his body!

At MacLaine's request, Mauricio removed his shirt to show he wasn't wired with any electrical device. During this brief lull, she told us that the first time she'd met him she had requested he strip to his shorts and stand in a pond of water to verify that he wasn't concealing electrical apparatus of any type.

Those of us sitting near the platform clearly observed the scarlet welts or scars forming on the center of Mauricio's forehead, throat, chest and abdomen during the evening as he continued to heal with the lights. "Chakra stigmata," MacLaine explained. "Notice that each is different. If you look closely, you can see the star of Enoch on his chest." Each stigma had a mark, as if from a branding iron. It was as if the red blemish had come from within, leaving the exterior scar.

For two hours Mauricio walked through the room, continuously healing and sending the light. He did it so often that it almost became commonplace. He seemed to know who needed his healing but didn't clarify how he knew it.

Many of us found ourselves in a quandary. While wishing to experience Mauricio's healing energy, we feared his attention would indicate that we had a serious ailment.

About midway through this extraordinary evening, he returned to the platform to drink water and lie down, positioning himself about five feet from where I was seated. With the approval of both Mauricio and MacLaine, I went to the platform and extended my hands over his prone body to sense his energy field.

There was no mistaking Mauricio's energy intensity. A strong, external force provided him with healing power, much like a supercharger provides added power to a race car. Although not threatening or fearful in any way, this energy definitely felt like it was not of this planet.

At one point during the evening, he approached our group, none of whom had yet been singled out for healing. When Mauricio leaned forward to heal a woman sitting directly behind us, Shirl instinctively grasped his arm to prevent his slipping off the dais; at the moment of contact, a flash exited his heart chakra and zapped the woman behind us. Although I'd seen this apparent miracle occur repeatedly, I was still startled.

"What did you feel?" I asked my wife as he moved on.

"A tingle, a pleasant sort of tingling in my hand and arm," she replied in a barely audible tone. She held her hand in front of her as if not knowing what to do with it. "It feels... soft."

After several hours Mauricio was exhausted, and Shirley MacLaine declared the evening session finished. She led her Brazilian guest to her bungalow so he could recover from his tiring ordeal.

Shirl asked the woman behind us if she knew why Mauricio had singled her out for healing. The woman explained that severe nerve damage had virtually immobilized her left arm, leaving her with restricted movement from shoulder to hand except for a few fingers. She said she saw the healing light go into her arm as if in slow motion.

"Tingly," was her response when someone sitting nearby asked her to describe the healing sensation. She didn't sense increased movement in the arm but felt a warm sensation, similar to the prickly feeling when an extremity has gone to sleep.

Shirl and I discussed the extraordinary events of the evening as we retreated to our dorm and the saggy, uncomfortable bunk beds which invariably accompany "rustic" retreat accommodations. We undressed to crawl into bed, still processing what we had just witnessed. Saying good night, I turned out the light and sprinted the six feet to my bunk, failing as always to reach the safety of the covers before the darkness completely overtook the room. I had no more settled in when I heard my wife shriek.

"Oh, my God, look at my hand!" she shouted.

I leaned over the edge of the bed and looked down. Her hand had a pale phosphorescent glow to it, unmistakable in the darkness. During the next 10 minutes we watched the glow gradually fade. Later, sleep took us, consigning consciousness to wherever it goes at night.

The next morning, her hand had returned to normal. During the predawn walk to the desert bluff where we met each morning for the daily sunrise meditation, we encountered the woman with the nerve-damaged arm who sat behind us the previous evening.

"How's the arm?" I asked hesitatingly, falling into stride beside her.

She stopped dead in her tracks. With tears of joy in her eyes, she lifted her arm freely over her head, wiggled her fingers and smiled into my eyes.

You didn't have to be a psychic to see her aura glowing in the predawn light!

CHAPTER 21

Secret Government Project

As people open themselves to new psychic or intuitive experiences, they begin to sense an expansion of self-awareness, as if a part of themselves had been newly awakened.

I'm not suggesting that this opening leads immediately to the "one-with-the-entire-universe" stage, but one generally begins to feel more connected to the larger "whole." This can be illustrated by the concept of "walk-ins"—people who suddenly sense a dramatically increased consciousness as if a more advanced energy had joined with their bodies. The old memories remain intact, yet there seems to be a newness of being at the same time.

Ever since my initial psychic episode, I began experiencing a "new" Chuck, and I found it difficult to share many of my new feelings, sensations and experiences with the social group that knew me before. Most of my friends weren't certain about the way to deal with someone who had dropped out of his first, 18-year marriage, then reemerged as a "psychic" with a new wife (since I met and married Shirl during the process).

It was as if I were living two lives, like a secret agent who maintains a hidden, parallel existence he cannot reveal even to his closest friends.

It was about this time that I was asked to participate in a psychic research project fronted by a graduate student from John F. Kennedy University but reportedly funded by the U.S. government!

Real secret agent stuff... how could I refuse?

The project would investigate the possibility that in ancient cultures the ruling elite may have used specific fragrances to alter the emotions of their citizenry in order to control their populations. Not surprisingly, this idea of control would attract the interest of certain folks in our government.

It is, of course, a well-known fact that sounds arouse emotions. When a military band plays "The Stars and Stripes Forever" march, or when monks chant, the sounds stir patriotic or reverent feelings, respectively. The simple vowel sounds of "eeeee," "ooooo" and "aahhh" in ancient mantras are believed to open and connect chakras.

A few years before, I witnessed a fascinating presentation—given by Dr. Jeffery Mishlove, the first individual to receive a doctorate in parapsychology from the University of California at Berkeley—on how sounds may have been influential in the lives of the ancient Peruvian culture.

Dr. Mishlove displayed to a group of metaphysicians 12 ancient clay pots recently discovered in an archaeological dig somewhere high in the Andes. These earthen vessels, however, were most unusual in appearance. Each had an identical long, curved, hollow handle, four or five times longer than the diameter of the bowl. The strange handles suggested that the pots were used for something other than cooking or carrying water. In fact, due to their unusually long and thin design, the handles would surely break off if even slight weight were placed in the pots.

Why would any culture form such apparently impractical pots?

Dr. Mishlove had discovered that if someone blew into the end of the handle, each pot would resonate a clear, distinctive tone. In fact, each of the dozen or so vessels in Dr. Mishlove's possession made one of *four* specific tones. Over time, Dr. Mishlove observed that certain combinations of tones predictably altered the mood of those listening to them.

With no further explanation, Dr. Mishlove selected 12 of us. We each held a pot which had been pre-numbered, one through four. We were told that vessels with identical numbers produced identical tones that were entirely distinct from the tones of the others.

He then instructed the three of us holding Peruvian pots identified by the number one to blow into the handles in turn. It reminded me of my high school band practice when we each would separately tune to the same specific chord.

He then suggested we blow into the handles again, but this time in unison. We took a deep breath, looked at each other to coordinate our timing and blew as instructed.

To our total amazement, no one could hear any sound at all!

Without prompting, we each took another big breath and blew again, only much harder.

There was *no* sound, nothing! Zip! Nada!

The three of us, blowing the same note at the same time, somehow canceled each other out!

Holding his hand up, and with a broad grin on his face, Dr. Mishlove dismissed our dumbfounded looks and went on to give us new instructions. He told us to be aware of our emotions as we listened to the six combinations of sounds that four pots could make when two of them emit tones simultaneously. He directed us to choose from the 10 emotions he had listed on a prepared handout.

Each of us, individually, wrote down the emotion we associated with each pair of possible tones. When we compared our reactions, the similarities were astounding. Maybe basic sounds *could* influence emotions.

So, could fragrances affect the emotions as well? Could past civilizations have used esoteric knowledge of fragrances to modify behavior? With these questions in mind, the J.F.K. research project sounded intriguing.

A few weeks after being asked to participate in the fragrance research project, a woman phoned to inform me that I was one of the six psychics chosen for this carefully controlled experiment. We would "read" identical fragrances and respond to an identical series of questions regarding each aroma.

When I inquired about the names of the other psychics or about details on how the tests were to be structured, she said they had not yet worked out the final details, but I would be fully informed at the appropriate time.

I expressed my willingness to take part on the condition that I be given procedural details up front and a copy of the results at the conclusion of the project.

"Of course," was her quiet, reassuring response.

Time went by, and I forgot all about the project when I did not hear anything further.

About six months later, the woman telephoned again and asked if I could meet one of their research staff members at a private home located in a remote section of town.

I reminded her that I still had a few concerns, but she assured me that all my questions would be answered. Intrigued by the secrecy surrounding this project, I agreed to the time and date suggested.

Following the directions mailed to me in an unmarked envelope, I drove to the address given. The house was set back from the road, well-hidden by tall, overgrown bushes. An attractive young woman greeted me at the front door and motioned me to follow her. As we walked down the hall, I noticed that most of the rooms were devoid of furniture, and I began to wonder what I had gotten myself into.

With few words, she led me to the far end of the house and into what she called the garden room. A myriad of large ferns hung beneath numerous skylights, and the room was wonderfully light and airy.

Gazing around this large, open space, I observed test tubes and scientific apparatus, much of it still in boxes scattered about. The only furniture in this room were a table and two chairs. These were placed near windows that overlooked a dry creek running through the large back yard.

She motioned me to sit while she busily set up the first experiment. I reminded her that I had really not committed to anything at this point and was here primarily to learn more about the project.

She responded that she didn't know anything about my previous conversations, but since I was here, why not work with one or two fragrances so I could experience firsthand what I was expected to do.

"Sure, why not," I thought aloud, "as long as I am here."

I was asked about 40 identical questions for each bouquet presented. Did this particular scent arouse passive or aggressive behavior? Could it aid physical healing? Did it increase one's awareness or motivate learning skills? Could it increase or decrease fertility? Could it be used to hypnotize or control?

By the end of the first session I was hooked.

I was scheduled for one meeting per week. At each session I was given two or three vials containing fragrances to test. Some were easily recognizable, such as sandalwood and cedar; other odors were totally foreign, obscure or downright repulsive.

I was told as little as necessary as the sessions continued. Details of the experimental procedures were not revealed, though I learned later that participating psychics progressed at their own, individual rate, never working for more than three hours at any one time. We were tested separately, and we were given no feedback during the process.

As I said earlier, I'd agreed to the experiment on the condition that I be given a copy of the written results of everyone's responses so I could compare my "hits" with those of the other participants. Psychics seldom miss an opportunity for such validating comparisons, since it is so difficult to obtain feedback on our work. For example, clients rarely provide verification on our predictions of future events. The police almost *never* tell us if the information we have provided has been helpful. Often, our only validation is from a returning client or a referral.

At the conclusion of the entire process, the promised comparative results of the research were never forthcoming! The lady who had contacted me left the university. I was told that the professor who fronted the experiment was on indefinite sabbatical leave. The university administration denied any knowledge of the study when questioned.

And the house where the work took place had been vacated!

Weeks later, I found that Gerri, my psychic mentor, was also one of the six psychics involved. She located a J.F.K. professor we believed knew about the experiment, but who flatly denied any knowledge of its results. When asked if the U.S. government participated, he suggested we just forget that the testing had ever occurred!

When Gerri and I learned of two other psychics who had participated in the project, we compared our remembrances, trying to establish results. We were all impressed with the similarities of our observations.

It is not surprising that this information has been suppressed. The U.S. government, at least publicly, has held that evidence for psychic phenomena—from spirit communication to telepathy to UFOs—is insupportable and therefore without value. Government research grants exploring this "science" are virtually unobtainable. Yet, it is interesting that this same government encouraged astronaut Edger Mitchell to experiment with telepathic transmissions to preselected viewers during an Apollo space mission.

Remember the 1986 Challenger shuttle rocket that exploded 73 seconds after takeoff, killing all seven of its crew members? Well, the dean of a northern California graduate school consciousness program has firsthand knowledge of a credible Michigan psychic who reported having received messages—the day after the explosion—from an entity identifying himself as the spirit of one of the departed astronauts. Within one week, all seven astronauts began channeling their individual messages through the documented trance state of this woman medium.

The deceased astronauts claimed they were brought together by non-physical guides and angels, including Seth, a well-documented spirit guide written about in a series of books by Jane Roberts. They reported that because the event had such an enormous impact on the planet's entire population, the seven found the collective strength to establish contact with the physical world. They wanted to testify to the existence of an afterlife, a fact that few of them had believed in before the cataclysmic event. Soon afterward, a second psychic, 2,000 miles away and without knowledge of the Michigan medium, began to receive identical information!

A research foundation in Mountain View, California, after verifying much of the personal data as highly accurate, became intrigued and applied for a grant through all available governmental funding channels. The U.S. government, to no one's surprise, was not the least bit interested.

So the foundation, at its own expense, brought both metaphysicians together and filmed fascinating dialogues between them and the non-physical spirits of the seven NASA astronauts. Several psychics who witnessed the public presentation of this material each "saw" the same astronauts standing alongside the presenter on various occasions.

It is a shame that we can spend taxpayers' money on a pork-barrel-freeway-to-nowhere or on some entrenched politician's pet boondoggle, but not on something that might enable us to reach higher states of consciousness and awareness.

It is also curious that Project Blue Book, the official, 10-year government study of tens of thousands of UFO sightings, should close due to "lack of evidence."

Lack of evidence?

The "Roswell Incident" was one of the first well-documented UFO cover-up stories. This event involved the crash of an unidentified flying object in Roswell, New Mexico, in 1947. The U.S. Air Force initially issued a press release stating, "The Wreckage Of A Flying Disk Has Been Recovered." Then, within hours, this statement was abruptly retracted. The fact that over 40 firsthand witnesses publicly stated they saw it, suggested that it was dismissed too quickly! No evidence?

Or, how about the claim of a cover-up by Bob Lazar, a well-known physicist/engineer, who stated that he was employed by the U.S. government at a top secret area, known as "S-4," located near Nellis Air Force Base in Nevada? He revealed that his job was to investigate the propulsion systems of recovered UFOs. He asserts that he examined nine different saucer-like craft, and he has publicly described the functioning of the antimatter generator used for propulsion. Impossible?

It is interesting that the three Apollo II astronauts (Neil Armstrong, Edwin Aldrin and Michael Collins) have publicly reported unexplainable paranormal sightings on the mission that landed men on the moon. Gemini XII astronauts claimed to have seen four UFOs linked together. *The Santa Cruz Sentinel* newspaper reported on April 17, 1974, that three Russian astronauts aboard a Vostod spacecraft said that they were surrounded by a "formation of fast-moving, disc-shaped objects."

President Ford, while still a member of Congress, was convinced enough to have insisted on a congressional investigation on UFOs. President Carter even confessed to having personally seen a UFO. President Johnson's secured telephone communications were severed at the same time the Air Force was tracking UFO formations and, simultaneously, trying to learn why both the power and the emergency generators at three Air Force bases and several civilian airports were unexplainably not operating. Senator Goldwater, the retired Air Force general and Republican presidential candidate in 1964, recently began his own investigation, but even he was denied access to these secret governmental files.

Hummmm... wonder why the U.S. government continues to keep these reports of the paranormal secret if they don't exist?

By contrast, the Russians have traditionally been active in exploring such paranormal subjects as psychokinesis (moving objects by thought), remote viewing (viewing distant objects as if they were within view) and out-of-body experiences (separating consciousness from the physical body). They also have discovered and developed the art of Kirlian photography—the process of capturing the entire energy image of an object on film *after* a portion of the object has been removed.

For many years, the old Soviet Union did not openly admit to their study of such psychic phenomena. Now that their society is more open, some Russian researchers have publicly discussed their findings. Hopefully, this knowledge, along with public interest, will lead to the declassification of information in our own country. Then perhaps we, the people whom our bureaucracy is designated to serve, may be told the truth and benefit from it.

I have direct knowledge of an intriguing, little-known event concerning our space program. Years ago, a government agency learned that "a certain foreign government" was attempting to scuttle our moon-landing program by the concentrated use of negative psychic energy.

Remember in the early sixties when the manned Apollo spacecraft was sent on a mission around the moon in preparation for the actual moon landing? What you may not recall was that the computers governing the rocket motors failed, and our nation held its collective breath while we worried about the fate of the astronauts. Only by maximizing the centrifugal force of the gravitational pull of the moon on the spacecraft were the astronauts eventually able to make a U-turn and return safely.

Well... the powers that be in Washington were concerned that this "other government" had used psychic energy to foul the electronics and computers and slow our progress in the race to the moon. The Central Intelligence Agency concluded that this foreign superpower probably had projected negative psychic vibes at our rocket ship.

Although our government officially denies the existence of psychic power, several American psychic practitioners were secretly flown to the NASA complex in Houston, at taxpayers' expense of course, during each subsequent moon shot! They were directed to deflect any negative psychic energy which may have been projected toward our space missions.

So, if you believe that our government has *not* found any "evidence" of flying saucers, extraterrestrials or paranormal events, then I have some great tideland property—suitable for immediate building—that I'd like to sell to you...

... CHEAP!

CHAPTER 22

First Police Case

It was at about this time that I cracked my first big case! (Well... maybe "cracked" isn't the definitive word; "stumbled through" might be a more appropriate phrase.)

One evening I received an unexpected telephone call from the police department in a neighboring city asking if I would help them on a case involving two missing children. The police inspector explained that they'd received my name from someone who thought I might be able to help. He wanted to know if he had the right Chuck Coburn. Personally, I have never known another Chuck Coburn, and I did not know where to start looking for another one at this late date.

I asked who had given him my name. He replied that he had first been given Gerri's name, who, in turn, suggested that he call me. He went on to add that he didn't personally believe in psychics, but he thought he would give it a shot since he had no substantial leads.

Not exactly a confidence-builder, but who was I not to try to help my community in its hour of need...?

I envisioned a future newspaper headline, "Local Psychic Nabs Kidnappers." Once the TV stations and wire services picked up the story, Hollywood would probably want to discuss motion picture rights. Would Robert Redford be right for my part, I wondered?

I asked him to give me some particulars.

One did not have to be the world's greatest mind reader to know from his tone that he was not exactly excited about requesting my assistance. He disclosed that the subjects were two brothers, one about 8 and the other 10, who were left in their mother's car while she ran into a store for "just a minute." When she returned, they were missing. He gave me their names and brief descriptions, and asked what else I needed.

I said that I preferred first to try to "pick up" something relevant and that I'd call him back later with whatever I got.

Hanging up the telephone I paused, then grabbed it again and immediately called Gerri. "You'll never guess who just called me," I shouted as she picked up the phone!

"What do you think, I'm psychic?" she jokingly responded. "So tell me... "

"Good luck," she sighed when I finished. "I won't work on any more police cases after my last experience."

She reminded me of her involvement with the San Francisco police years before during a murder case that received national media attention. Although she had insisted on anonymity, her name was released somehow, and she had received numerous threatening notes and phone calls. The police never provided her with feedback and seemed unconcerned for her safety. She suggested I request that my name not be released publicly.

Maybe I wouldn't be around to see who played my role in the motion picture after all.

I informed Gerri that I had told the police inspector that I would at least give it a shot. But, between his negative attitude and Gerri's experience, I almost hoped that nothing would come from my involvement.

I hung up the phone and took a deep breath, deciding that if I were to go on, it would be for the sake of an anxious mother, not for the fulfillment of my ego. Then I asked my guides to provide a visualization of the car, kids, parking lot, etc.—anything that would help me determine what had taken place.

I closed my eyes and waited.

After several moments, I envisioned an aerial-view panorama of a shopping center parking lot, just as I'd seen in a dramatic scene from an old Alfred Hitchcock movie. There were numerous vehicles and movements, but before the camera got close enough to identify anything specific, the scene froze, as if the pause button had been pressed on a VCR.

I replayed the scene over and over in my mind, but all I saw was a parking lot, assorted automobiles, light standards, directional signs and a clock tower off to one side. The hands of the clock were pointing to 1:30.

The more I attempted to locate something specific, the more diffused the picture became. I decided to call the police inspector back and tell him I wasn't getting anything specific.

"Well, did you see anything?" he asked, his voice showing indications of a long, hard day. I told him I was sorry, but I couldn't come up with anything other than a large parking lot. He asked me to describe the lot.

"It's just a large parking lot," I answered, and I related the few details I could recall, including the large clock tower.

"Describe the clock and tower," he commanded, a little more interested.

I told him that it was a tall, wooden structure with several X-shaped braces; that it supported a large, multicolored clock face with its hands positioned at 1:30.

"Funny you should say that... ," he said softly.

He confided that although there was no tower, there *was* a large clock on the side of the building adjacent to the area where the mother's car had been parked. "Wait a minute," he whispered, and the phone line went dead as if I had been put on hold.

He came back minutes later and disclosed that the report in front of him showed that the kids were discovered missing at... *1:30!* There was more patience in his voice now, and he asked if I would work further on this case.

I hung up, electrified by my success, while aware of a new sense of urgency and pressure. What if I could not get anything more? What if I were wrong?

Psychics are judged to be as good as their last statement. I knew my credibility would be evaluated by my next pronouncement, despite the number of correct hits which may have preceded it.

I closed my eyes and again waited for my guides to feed me psychic impressions.

After a few moments, an incredibly peaceful country setting appeared in my mind's eye. It reminded me of the opening scene of the movie *The Sound of Music*, when the camera pulls back from the close-up shot of Julie Andrews dancing on the crest of a hill and reveals the beautiful, grass-covered valley beyond. I looked down the slope into the bowl of my valley, but I saw no houses, roads or even people.

I tried to work the kidnapped boys into this picture, but the more I attempted to force the visualization, the more fuzzy it became. So I left it and went to bed.

The next morning I awoke, vividly recalling dreams of this same valley where I observed it from several different angles, as if I were reviewing a number of still photographs. There was a message here I was sure, but what? Where was this generic valley? No landmarks or names identified its location. There had been no sign of the children.

After wrestling with this puzzle for most of the morning, I called the police inspector and admitted that I was stymied.

"The only impression I had was a grass valley," I conceded, "and I have no idea where it is."

"In northern California, above Sacramento," he replied with a touch of sarcasm in his voice.

"No," I said, "I was referring to an unidentified, grass-covered valley," and I went on to describe it from the various perspectives that I had envisioned. "No kids, though."

"Grass Valley is the name of a city up north," he repeated; "matter of fact, I have a brother-in-law on the police force there."

I stated that I was sorry at not being of any more help and politely ended the call.

Unable to dismiss my concern for the children, I called the police about a week later. The inspector was not in, but another officer working on the case told me the boys had just been found that same morning, and the bad guys had been arrested. That's all he would reveal.

Wanting to at least know *where* the children had been located, I tracked down the inspector in his office several days later.

He told me that he couldn't release details because the case was not yet closed, but he confided that they had been abducted by their father and then escaped on their own.

"Just one more question," I begged. "Can you just tell me *where* they were found? Was it near a large grassy valley by any chance?"

Then, after an awkward silence, he told me.

"They were found *in* Grass Valley... *Grass Valley, California!*"

(Freddy the Pig would have been proud!)

How many times do we discount feelings or intuitive flashes because our logic gets in the way? "The car *couldn't* be near a clock tower because I am not aware of any clock tower matching that description."

And how many times do we misinterpret or ignore what we intuit? "I see a grass valley, but since the impressions are vague or illogical, the information must be valueless."

My wife, Shirl, is a dream facilitator; she teaches her clients how to make sense of their nighttime adventures so they can comprehend for themselves the meaning and message of their dreams. Because dream symbols have a specific meaning known only to the dreamer, she rarely tells them what their dream symbols mean. Instead, she provides a procedure to help them discover their own meanings. In most instances, the dream images *cannot* be interpreted literally.

Since a psychic or intuitive visualization is very much like a dream, the same rules apply. In my reading of the kidnapping case, my grass valley was *not* just a valley covered with grass. Instead, it was Grass Valley, a California town. The information was correct; the symbol merely required a different interpretation.

Shirl had a dream one night about a green string coming out of her nose; the string was attached to some bacon she was frying on the stove. Not your standard run-of-the-mill dream, but as she began to analyze it, she understood the symbolism. She was concerned about a career change, and the dream provided resolution. The answer was "as plain as the *nose* on her face" but there was a "*string* attached" to "bringing home the *bacon.*" The dream had a very definite message once she understood the code. Her dream message had been delivered in metaphors.

An intuitive understanding—arising from a psychic flash, a moment of inspiration, a *déjà vu* experience, channeled knowing, an impulsive idea, an angel whisper or an informative dream—is, basically, a momentarily altered state of consciousness. It differs substantially from a normal state of awareness.

Because intuitive messages originate from a "different place," their form or language may seem peculiar or unusual, but each of us can learn to understand it if we will only open ourselves to the experience. The problem is that our doubting nature intercedes, and we often end up misinterpreting or ignoring the intuitive data. Frequently our psychic processes provide us valid information, but we fail to recognize it.

As in a dream, we may view psychic data in a variety of modes before recognizing the meaning. However, once we are willing to look hard enough, we can find it. Once we trust our discoveries, it becomes much easier to identify and interpret subsequent intuitive or psychic messages.

Remember, since each of us is an individual, we often experience the same things differently.

- Some people perceive psychic information best by "visualizing"; others, by "hearing."
- Some people have greater accuracy with first psychic impressions; others have better results following long-term meditations.
- Some find their psychic energy works best spontaneously; others must consciously focus at a predetermined time and place.

- Some people are more successful working in the present moment; others have greater success looking to the future or the past.

If you wish to develop your psychic ability and intuitiveness, begin to pay attention to what, how and when you do your best.

And when you gain the necessary confidence, know that you *already* know the information you are seeking. Who knows, given enough practice and encouragement, you just might get good at it!

CHAPTER 23

Remote Viewing

The overwhelming majority of my private readings have been for those who were sympathetic to the phenomenon and open to the experience. Following my involvement with the law enforcement agency, I realized just how difficult it is to psychically read people who are cynical and unbelieving.

Skepticism is healthy, but there is little to be gained in working with entrenched nonbelievers who only want to prove you wrong and frustrate you. Not much is achieved by either party from such confrontations. Early on I learned to avoid rigid skeptics, in part by charging a nominal fee that kept such people at a distance.

Once, soon after I had actively begun to give psychic readings to the public, I encountered a client at a social gathering. She introduced me to her husband, specifically mentioning that I was the psychic who had given her a reading.

His body language unmistakably informed me that he didn't believe in "that stuff." Puffing up his chest and winking at several of his friends, he questioned in a loud and challenging voice, "Well, if you are such a damn good psychic, tell me what I had for lunch today?"

After the laughter subsided, I calmly explained that it didn't work quite that way and this was *not* the proper time or place for a reading. Bolstered by his audience, he refused to drop the subject and continued to bring the conversation back to the same question. With additional pairs of eyes now focused on me, I didn't know how to gracefully extricate myself short of providing a brief demonstration.

Gathering all the confidence I could muster and hoping my spirit guides were in the vicinity, I called upon them for assistance. Then I heard myself telling my challenger that he had visited a new place for lunch, adding that it was an Italian deli with a blue awning mounted over the entry on which the name of the establishment was displayed in fancy white script!

All eyes moved to him.

Without a word of acknowledgment, he gave me an overly patient grin and softly repeated, "I asked you *what* I had for lunch today."

The eyes shifted back to me.

It was interesting how much warmer the room had suddenly become. My inquisitor was not about to give an inch, and I couldn't believe that I had allowed myself to be maneuvered into this situation. I looked up on the off chance that one of my guides had written something on the ceiling or that I would discover an idea in one of those little, cloud-shaped conversation bubbles which appear over the heads of cartoon characters, but to no avail.

Opening my mouth again, I heard myself reporting, "You had a pastrami sandwich on rye and a cup of coffee, black, no cream or sugar!"

All sets of eyes moved back to him as if watching a tennis

match. The ball was now in *his* court, but I had no idea if it was inbounds or not.

"With mayonnaise or mustard?" he retorted, his face devoid of expression.

"Mustard," I blurted out, most likely reacting more than psychically viewing.

"NO," he proudly exclaimed, "mayonnaise *and* mustard!" He chuckled and abruptly walked away, quite pleased with himself.

To my expanding list of people a psychic should not read, I added "doubting husbands at cocktail parties!"

The lesson? It is tough to be tested because such testing arouses everyone's ego. In this case, it was my pride against his credibility with his friends. Most psychics do not allow themselves to be tested by *any* person or group—research scientists in particular—for several reasons.

First, the mere fact that a psychic is being observed, tested and judged changes the energy of the event, as demonstrated by the quantum physics theory which states that the observed is altered by the observer. It is not unlike being on trial in a court of law, except that the burden of proof is on the psychic! In such a situation, psychics submit to great pressure, and they risk losing their personal credibility.

Also, those who conduct tests, especially scientific ones, test in *their* sterile environment, using *their* methods, at *their* timing, with *their* equipment. There is little to gain by attempting to prove the existence of psychic events with inflexible, scientific measuring tools, particularly when many investigators are more intent on *disproving* psychic phenomena than analyzing or validating them.

Stanford Research Institute in Palo Alto, California, is one of the few exceptions. Researchers there explore the outer limits of known psychic abilities to understand, not challenge their existence. S.R.I. has documented some fascinating studies of psychic events, two of which I have experienced personally: remote viewing and precognition.

The first, remote viewing, involves observing something beyond the range of normal vision. In an S.R.I. sleep laboratory, volunteers with proven paranormal abilities are encouraged to journey out-of-body while asleep. In one of the experiments, researchers create a 10-digit number using a random number generator and place it face-up on a high shelf near the ceiling. The sleep volunteer is instructed to exit his or her body while asleep, read the number on the shelf and report it upon awakening. Many volunteers have read several digits of the target number correctly, exceeding the laws of chance by a *wide* margin. Some can consistently recall the entire 10 digits without error!

During a retreat directed by several psychic researchers who conducted many of these experiments at S.R.I., I experienced a variation of this process. We were sequestered in condominiums in Pajaro Dunes, a remote beach community located along a foggy coastline in central California.

Late one evening, just before retiring for the night, we were informed that certain objects would be placed on the roof of a specified unit. We were instructed to go to sleep, then float above the roof in our spiritual bodies and observe the objects we found on the roof.

Upon awaking the next morning, I recalled what I traditionally would have described as a dream, except that it was more like a waking event. In the "dream" I flew leisurely over an endlessly long strip of black, sandy beach. I could clearly see a small, round, solid platform off to one side. On it rested a dark box, about the size of a shoebox, with a ridged, dark handle spanning its length.

After reporting our experiences the next morning, we

were shown our target objects: an old-fashioned, black flat-iron with a long, ridged black handle. The previous night it had been placed on the round seat of a three-legged, wooden stool on the roof.

Was I wrong? Well, when observed from directly above, the flatiron and circular seat closely resembled—in shape, size and color—a shoebox and round platform.

Was it a dream or an out-of-body remote viewing? It didn't matter. The fact was that I trusted the process and was rewarded with confirmation of a psychic experience.

Remember, the psychic abilities each of us inherently possesses are virtually limitless! The first step is to believe they are accessible!

Another S.R.I. remote viewing experiment involves two subjects working closely together. The first person, designated as the "sender," is asked to select an envelope from a collection of sealed envelopes which contain the names of preselected landmarks located within a short driving distance. This sender is then instructed to drive off the S.R.I. campus, open the envelope and travel immediately to the designated location.

At an agreed-upon time, the sender focuses his attention directly on the landmark in front of him. At the same moment, the second person, the "receiver," attempts to draw the image the sender is observing. Some of the results are startlingly accurate and have been widely reported in various publications.

Precognition, the second psychic study that I am familiar with at S.R.I., refers to knowing or viewing a specific future event *prior* to its occurrence.

During the Pajaro Dunes weekend, we also participated

in a precognition experiment. This time, we were not working within present time as we had during the remote viewing study. Instead, we were to observe an event which would occur in the *future*.

Initially, we were shown a short video in which an S.R.I. researcher, unknown to any of us, described an experiment we could undertake with him. The man in the video explained that we could try to determine at 10:00 A.M. this same morning exactly where he would be and what he would be doing at noon, *two hours later!* He told us that he would be more than 200 miles away from our California location and that no one connected with our seminar would know his whereabouts.

Precisely at 10:00 A.M., our retreat instructor led us through a guided meditation to raise our state of awareness. He repeatedly assured us that we each had the ability to "remember the future." At the conclusion of this meditation, we were given pencil and paper and asked to follow the verbal instructions he would present.

While focusing on a photograph of the person in the video, we answered questions targeting the "where" and "what" of his noontime activity. "Be a receiver, not a judge," we were reminded repeatedly, as we wrote down any words, impressions or symbols which appeared to our consciousness, regardless of their apparent relevancy.

My own sketches included images that resembled birds and a series of vertical lines with two horizontal lines running through them, like rails laid off-center on very long railroad ties. I had also sketched an image, wide at the bottom and narrowing to a point at the top, which could be a rounded door or window, and I had repeatedly written the words "St. Louis" at the top of my paper.

I speculated that our target might go to the St. Louis Zoo, perhaps to a bird aviary, with the "railroad tracks" actually representing the bars of a cage.

When we compared notes during the break that followed, five of the 25 participants in the experiment had also written down the words "St. Louis!" No question... he was in St. Louis. He had to be!

At 12:30 P.M., our precognitive subject telephoned, and the speaker phone was activated so all of us could hear.

"Where are you?" we shouted in unison.

"New Orleans" was his response—there was a chorus of disappointed groans! "I'm in New Orleans," he repeated, "and at noon I was standing in the center of a large plaza, facing a large cathedral, feeding the pigeons."

Birds! I had gotten the birds!

He went on to describe the adjacent area which included a wrought iron fence, its vertical pickets supported by two continuously running, horizontal bars.

My railroad tracks!

In answer to someone's request to describe the outer appearance of the cathedral, he mentioned the unique window over the entry. Chills ran up and down my body as I heard him specifically delineate my *wide at the bottom and pointed at the top* image!

Although absolutely thrilled at the accuracy of my impressions, I was surprised that I had misidentified his location, particularly since a fifth of our group had written the words "St. Louis."

As our long-distance conversation was drawing to a close, one disappointed woman said she had been certain he was in St. Louis and reported that several others had come to a similar conclusion.

There was a momentary silence, followed by a knowing chuckle. "Oh," he said softly, "I guess I forgot to mention that the church I was focusing on was the *St. Louis Cathedral.*"

Had we not been with experienced seminar leaders, we might have dismissed some of our hits as misses. Only by examining the results with their assistance did we conclude that many of our intuitions were valid.

And don't we routinely do that all the time? How often do we *know* something, but dismiss it as illogical or coincidental? How many times do we "have a feeling," but ignore it as "only a feeling?"

Instead of denying our experiences, how about asking ourselves two key questions:

First, "Can I do it?"

Second, "Am I willing to take the risk?"

(Since this is not a high school math text and the answers cannot be found at the back of this book, I'll tell you now that the correct response to both questions is a resounding YES!)

CHAPTER 24

The Reward

As we become more trusting of developing our psychic tools, we begin to appreciate their full potential. When we use them to save someone's life, we realize they are *priceless!*

Some years ago I received a telephone call from a metaphysical colleague who assists various national governmental agencies with her psychic gifts. She informed me that the Federal Aviation Agency had requested her assistance in locating a missing private aircraft. The plane had apparently been downed by a sudden snowstorm in Oregon, and the airplane's transponder, which generally emits a directional radio signal upon impact, had malfunctioned. Because of the occasional, faint sound of children crying heard on a radio frequency used exclusively by private pilots, the F.A.A. thought there were survivors.

Most psychics agree that knowing facts and information about a situation can lead to assumptions which hinder intuitive knowing, and my friend felt that her familiarity with the area was interfering in this way. Since I had no knowledge or emotional connection with the terrain, she reasoned that I might help fill a few gaps.

Sharing none of the specific data she had received through the F.A.A. or her channeling, she provided me only with what I needed to know. I created the necessary "space." The process is somewhat like saying, in my imagination, "If I could tap into the consciousness of what had happened, it might be as follows... ," and then allowing a higher guidance to complete the story.

As I gave myself permission to "remember," I picked up individual and disjointed pieces of information, such as possible compass directions, unfamiliar names and random numbers. I took care *not* to edit or sort the information, nor did I attempt to construct any conclusions.

Some of my impressions were visual, like numbers appearing on a blackboard in a specific sequence or views of a three-dimensional relief map. Others were auditory, similar to remembering a friend's voice repeating a phone number.

I called my colleague back, and we compared notes. Some of the numbers we had collected were identical. I verified her hits on the words "south" and "west" since I had a strong impression that the plane was downed in the lower left corner of the state. Upon referring to a map, we discovered that two of the numbers were portions of latitude and longitude coordinates intersecting in the lower left or *southwest* part of the state!

She came up with a word which might be the name of a town, river or geographical point. I had received a number which I reasoned could be an elevation. Upon checking further, we determined that her word coincided with the name of a mountain, and my number, if it were an elevation, might pinpoint a specific location.

As we were to learn, the reading was the easy part. Convincing the authorities was much more difficult!

The official search currently under way was determined by the pilot's preflight plan and centered about 125 miles to the northeast of the position we ascertained. The F.A.A. informed us that our determination wasn't logical and that they would not divert their search planes on a "wild goose chase."

"Thanks, but *no* thanks" was basically what they were saying.

Several days later, the wire services carried a report that two children had been rescued from a crashed plane near a remote mountainside in Oregon. Investigating further, we learned that they were found *within several miles of the location we had drawn on our map!*

According to the news report, an air controller had alerted a private pilot that there might be a downed aircraft in his vicinity. While flying around the seldom traveled backside of the mountain, he spotted the debris. The pilot later stated he would most likely *not* have seen it had he not been watchful as a result of the air controller's alert.

Someone had heard us after all!

Did we feel cheated? No, not at all. We were glad to have had a small part in the timely rescue of two small kids!

Did we ever get another call from the F.A.A.? Are you kidding?

I was involved with another airplane incident, this one concerning my brother-in-law. Some years ago during a telephone conversation, he casually mentioned that he had a "funny feeling" about scheduling a business trip to Philadelphia. Since he had me on the phone, he wanted my psychic input. I responded by saying I would work on it, but my first impression was Philadelphia felt O.K.

I called him back later that evening to inform him that my guides had told me that he should *not* go to Chicago.

He informed me that he had no business in Chicago and his question was regarding a trip to Philadelphia.

I repeated what I had been told which was that he should *not go to Chicago.*

"Read my lips, Philadelphia, P-h-i-l-a-d-e-l-p-h-i-a," he responded slowly with a forced patience that I could feel on my end of the phone.

I said, "Norm, all I can tell you is do not go to Chicago. Perhaps the meeting will be relocated or will require a follow-up trip to Chicago. I don't know, but I would strongly advise you to stay clear of Chicago."

About a week later I received another telephone call from Norm.

"I am scheduled to leave for Philadelphia tomorrow morning, but when reviewing my airline tickets I discovered that my travel agent has me routed home *through Chicago.* What do you think I should do?"

My response again was that my spiritual counsel seemed very clear about avoiding Chicago.

Because of our conversation, he canceled the trip!

Several days later he learned that the airplane, which would have taken him from Chicago back to Los Angeles, *crashed* moments after takeoff, killing over 300 of those aboard!

Your guides will *never* present you with inappropriate information. Psychic information, *lovingly* channeled from your higher consciousness, is *always* pertinent to your growth or it would not have been presented to you in the first place. On a deep subconscious level, you already know much of it.

I seldom perceive negative events when channeling for clients because I have learned that my guides only present information that might be helpful to the person receiving it. The recipient is then free to make the necessary changes to alter a *potential* future that would not serve his or her greater need. That is what free will is all about. In Norm's case, once he understood the communication with his higher self, he was free to modify the outcome.

Once we become aware of the presence of our higher guides, we can begin to recognize and eventually modify the means by which they deliver their information. It's similar to programming a crystal or a computer. We can determine the "how," "what" and "when" of their communication simply by our expectation.

There are several ways through which you can initiate contact.

1. Meditation. Locate your quiet place inside and request your higher self, or guide(s), to communicate with you in the form of individual words, thoughts or ideas.

Expect to receive the information they would like you to have!

2. At a predetermined time each morning, know that your guides will provide you with a specific, meaningful word for the day. Count down from five to one and *know* that you will see or hear a word or short phrase as you reach the final number. Try to see the word in a written form if you learn by seeing. If you learn by hearing, listen for it. Or, perhaps, try to just "know" the word.

And then don't try; just do it!

3. Alter your consciousness by bringing yourself to a relaxed state of mind—which *is* an altered state of consciousness—and ask a question. Visualize a movie screen or blackboard in your mind's eye. See the lights dim and curtains part, and *allow* the movie to begin.

You do *not* have to "see" your guides face-to-face to benefit from their guidance!

4. Request guidance by consulting oracles, such as the *I Ching,* runes or tarot cards. Allow your spirit guides to answer your inquiries and provide appropriate information and insights. I'm not suggesting that you make major decisions solely by selecting a stone or card. However, you *can* access subtle guidance from a perspective beyond the logical processes on which we too often rely for direction.

Try it! You'll be well rewarded for your efforts.

5. Work with a pendulum. A pendulum can provide reliable yes or no answers to questions, once you have learned to trust it. Create your own pendulum by tying a crystal to the end of a light thread and then ask it questions you know are answered yes. Next, observe how differently it responds to questions you know must be answered with a no. Once you have discerned the range of its individual movements, it is programmed. Now ask it questions of which you are less certain.

Be open to the information you receive. Learn to trust the answers. The more you trust it, the more it works.

6. Once you have mastered the crystal pendulum, *become* a pendulum. Stand perfectly erect, as if you

could easily be moved by a feather, and ask obvious, yes/no questions. Note the almost imperceptible nudge your guides give you, as if they were standing alongside. They will nudge you in one direction for yes and in another for no. Program the direction, much like you did with your crystal pendulum. I guarantee that the answers you receive will help you!

7. Ask a question of your guides before you drift off to sleep and *expect* an answer. Your guides may provide insight in a dream or in your waking life. For example, if you ask where you should go on vacation, in the following days your attention might be drawn to a billboard that promotes a specific vacation locale. You then might hear from a friend who just returned from this identical location and encourages you to go. Then you might flip a magazine open to photographs of the very same locale! It's the old synchronicity idea. Remember coincidences?

8. *Know* that your guides are working with you whether you are consciously aware of them or not. They are here to serve *you*. If you are serious about meeting them, they will make themselves known to you; just watch for them.

    When you ask your guides a question, be careful how you phrase it. "Which vacation shall I take?" can be answered from several different perspectives. Are you asking which vacation would be most fun or which would be the most economical or which would be the most relaxing?

Be specific or you most certainly will receive mixed messages.

Funny You Should Say That…

And remember: Be careful what you ask for…

You just might get it!

CHAPTER 25

The Three M's

This seems to be an appropriate place to introduce you to what I call The Three M's.

MEDITATION—

First, let's examine the import of meditation. Although I've referred to it in previous chapters as a means by which we might meet our guides or higher self, some clarification might be helpful.

Meditation is simply a method of tuning in to the small voice within: *your truth.* You may label this voice or source the Christ Consciousness, the God Within, or even the Universal Force. Whatever the label, it is your individual method of knowing what truly is. Christ said that the kingdom of God is found by going within, and *that* process is, basically, meditation.

Meditation often gets a bad rap because many folks

unfamiliar with the practice imagine that it's a mysterious ritual undertaken by weird people who sit in the lotus position while dressed in unconventional clothing.

In truth, meditation is similar to prayer, except that instead of speaking with a separate, external entity, we speak with—or become one with—our inner source. In meditation, we create a quiet setting in order to seek our *own* truth directly from a higher counsel. When we meditate, we do not depend on anyone else's interpretation, but only on our own.

So, the first question might be: What is the *best* procedure to follow in order to meditate?

The answer is: Do whatever works for you.

Traditionally, people sit motionlessly in a comfortable position and in a peaceful environment with the aim of gaining insight or inspiration from the quiet place within. Until you discover your personal style, I recommend the following technique because it provides a structured guideline.

Divide your meditation into two phases. First, position your body in a comfortable but erect position with your hands folded in your lap and your head tilted slightly downward. Place your attention on a mantra, which is, basically, a single, focused thought-sound. The *American Heritage Dictionary* defines mantra as a sacred verbal formula repeated in prayer, meditation, or incantation, such as an invocation of a god, a magic spell or a syllable or portion of scripture containing mystical potentialities.

Commonly, meditators repeat the sound "Oooommmmmmmm" as their mantra. You can also listen to soothing music, smell a rose or stare into a candle flame. You can observe water trickling over stones in a creek or focus on the rhythm of your breathing. All such methods will help clear the mind and allow you to "get out of your head." If outside thoughts intrude, acknowledge them and just let them pass through your consciousness and exit without effort. At the same time, sense the center of your body as the midpoint of your awareness.

In the second phase of your meditation, release your hands and open them in your lap, palms facing up, with thumb and forefinger or middle finger forming an O. This will help you retain and circulate your energy. Lift your head slightly as if you were about to engage in a new channel of communication from above. Feel your throat and heart chakras open as you pave a new roadway for incoming information.

Think of your abdomen as the focal point for these new messages. Allow new, increased knowing to enter your body through your crown chakra or third eye and move downward, registering in your center rather than in your head, where we all have been previously taught to think things through.

As you become comfortable with this process, imagine that your guides are in the vicinity. Invite them to come closer; ask them to come into your space. Acknowledge their presence and allow them to assist you. They will be much more communicative if they know you are heeding their advice!

As you go inside to your quiet place—your center— you may see images or hear voice patterns or sense energies that previously have gone unnoticed.

Some people find it helpful to envision a material object, such as a stereo receiver/amplifier, TV screen or message center, to help them receive this insight. Others might think, "If I could hear something, what would it be?" Listen to incoming messages from your guides with your heart, not with your ears; hear the message from *inside*.

As you become more comfortable with this process, you might soon trust yourself to ask questions. When you do, you will begin to receive answers.

Don't try too hard! Later on, don't try at all. Just *allow* the experience to happen. And don't give up. Hey, you didn't learn to ride your bike without falling, did you?

Any altered state of consciousness is, essentially, a form of meditation. When you are daydreaming or drifting off to sleep, you are experiencing a form of meditation. Once you have gained success with the more formal approach, you will receive guidance from your higher spiritual source at mundane, routine times, as you are waiting for a bus or washing the dishes.

Gradually you will develop the capability of contacting your guides by recalling and repeating the emotional or bodily sensations which accompanied your initial experience.

MANIFESTATION—

Ever heard of a concept known as "creating a parking place?" It's the old, familiar power of positive thinking idea, and it goes like this. Let's say you are late for an appointment and you don't have time to hunt for a place to park. If you understand the metaphysical process, you can simply create a parking place by believing one will be available and just waiting for you. Similarly, if you are certain that there will not be any place to park, there probably won't be. "See, I told you so; I'm not lucky!"

Think back. How many times when you *really* needed something did it show up, particularly when you didn't have the time to doubt that it would be there?

To further illustrate this notion, let me relate a personal experience. Sometime ago I had arranged to meet a friend for dinner at a restaurant in a densely populated section of a large city. I knew it would be hard to find parking there, especially at that time of day, so I worked throughout the afternoon on "creating" a parking place directly in front of our destination.

As I arrived, I saw an empty parking space on the other side of the busy, two-way street right in front of the restaurant! Pleased with myself, I made a U-turn at the intersection and came back to claim my place. At that moment, the lady I was to meet backed *her* car into *my* parking spot.

It took me 20 minutes to find another place to park! When I finally walked into the restaurant, my friend shot me one of those "you're late" looks. I apologized, but quickly explained that I was late because *she* had taken *my* parking place, the one I had so deliberately brought into being.

She said that I was mistaken. She had also imaged *her* parking place in front of the restaurant. But, she added with a wry smile, the difference was that she had manifested the space *with her car in it!*

Minor details! They sometimes forget to tell you that part!

And how about the people we label lucky? Have you ever really wanted to attend an event but couldn't purchase a ticket because it was sold out, while your friend was given a free ticket… in the front row?

Maybe your friend wasn't necessarily lucky but just a *good creator!*

As mentioned earlier, enlightened masters have taught that, in effect, we each create our own reality. Our guides, wishing to please us, receive our thought-energy and create for us exactly what we think or what we believe. If we believe we are unlucky, they simply arrange bad luck to please us!

So… if we just change our thinking…

There are, of course, many people who do not choose to believe that we create everything that happens to and for us. To those people I can only say, "O.K., *your* belief system is *your* reality; you believe your beliefs and they will be true for you."

Meanwhile, I will believe mine. (And may we each be tolerant enough to allow the other to peacefully *believe* or *think* freely.)

Some who do subscribe to this basic law of creation become confused when the process doesn't work with any consistency. If you are one of those, I will let you in on a little secret: *there are three basic steps to manifestation!*

1. The first step is to *know what you want!*

When you enter a restaurant, for example, you cannot *get* what you want until you *know* what it is that you want. How can the waitperson bring you what you wish to eat until you clearly know it yourself? The same concept applies to manifestation. When you ask for what you want, be clear and be specific because if you entertain confusing or inconsistent thoughts, confusion is what your spiritual guides will likely provide you!

And thoughtfully consider your long-range desires— what it is you *really* desire!

If, for example, you think happiness is achieved by earning a pile of money to purchase a boat in order to experience freedom, don't create the money and don't even bother with the boat. Create what the boat will provide you. *Create the freedom!* You may be limiting yourself by focusing on the money or the boat and not on the freedom! There may be a more direct way to obtain what you really want than the way you imagine.

2. The second step in manifesting what you want is to

know that you have it!

Don't hope you can get it; don't wish you had it; *know* that you already possess it. For example, if you desire to be promoted to a specific corporate position, *know* that it is yours. Start planning on what you will do *when* you get the position, not *if* you get it. Visualize yourself sitting in the chair at your new desk. Go out and buy new clothing that goes with your new position!

Function as if you have already received what it is that you wish to create. See *yourself* in the corporate chair prior to receiving the corporate position. As contrary as it may sound, you cannot obtain something until you already possess it. Like love: to truly experience love with another, you must first have love for yourself.

Returning to the restaurant example, you have decided what you want and placed your order. Now, don't you assume the food is virtually yours? Don't you picture it in front of you? Can't you taste it? (Children are so good at this that they can't understand why it doesn't show up immediately!)

3. Step three is to *let go*—get out of the way and *let it happen!*

You have placed your order; you know the food is yours. Now, don't place obstacles in the way of the server bringing the food to you. "What if I *don't* get it? What if *they* give it to someone else?" Those thoughts can completely undermine all the positive actions taken in the first and second steps.

If passengers in my car actively challenge the viability of my creating a parking space, I sometimes become defensive and end up creating doubt and uncertainty. In order to defend my ego, I might say, "It *usually* works, but it may not today." Then I have lost the positive thought required to manifest what I want.

So, (1) decide what you want; (2) know that you have it; then (3) let go of undermining thoughts that arise from doubt or ego and let your creation happen! This simple three-step procedure will eliminate many self-defeating blocks which have prevented you from successfully manifesting your goals.

MARSHMALLOWS—

We have considered Meditation and Manifestation. Finally we come to the last of the three M's—Marshmallows.

What are marshmallows, you ask? Well, marshmallows are the little puffy white things that you place on the end of a stick when you sit around a campfire and sing songs you wouldn't sing anywhere else.

What do *marshmallows* have to do with meditation or manifestation? Not much…

Why did I include *marshmallows* in my list of the Three M's? Because I only had two M's and I needed one more…

CHAPTER 26

Sacred Power Sites

People all over our planet are beginning to rediscover an antiquated truth that has been all but forgotten in this modern era. We no longer build our own shelters and hunt or raise our own food. We, instead, depend on our rapidly advancing society to take care of such tasks. As a result, we have forgotten how to take care of ourselves. Unfortunately, we have even forgotten how to get to our own *truth*, but that truth is where it has always been… *inside*.

Remember, we are primarily energy beings, enjoying a brief romp in physical form! Since the Supreme Being created us out of the Absolute Perfection of Itself, we are more truly eternal, cosmic or spiritual energy forms than temporary, physical bodies. The earth-suit we inhabit is merely a momentary reflection or aspect of our eternal being, a temporarily separate and individual consciousness.

One effective method of augmenting our contact with the inner spiritual energy is to visit natural, sacred energy power sites, which are scattered throughout our physical world. Each site offers a unique experience. Many sites retain their original power and can accelerate the opening of our higher consciousness in the same way they did for ancient peoples.

So, let's again go back to those thrilling days of yesteryear and examine a few of the ancient power spots that remain today.

In ancient Greece, the female priestess known as the Oracle of Delphi provided answers to those who traveled great distances seeking her wisdom. She spoke to them while in trance, an altered state of consciousness reached by inhaling the fumes emanating from the caverns below her perch on a raised rock. Rulers and heads of state often sought her counsel before making grave decisions that ultimately affected world history.

Why? Why would some of the most powerful world leaders journey to the top of a remote mountain to seek information from a woman who was obviously high on a hallucinatory drug? Did the Oracle have a direct link to the source of truth?

One has to assume she did, or leaders wouldn't have made the arduous trek to seek her advice. After all, these were men of intelligence who had reached and maintained lofty positions of power.

If you travel to where the Oracle resided in Delphi, Greece, you may still sense the energy and commanding force neglected and forgotten by modern man. Yin-passive and yang-power serenely commingle at this location. Having lain dormant for such a long period, this energy is peaceful, yet strong, explosive and restless; it is the same energy that fueled the preliminary stages of Christianity and Democracy.

Spiritual energy can also be found in many ancient temples on the banks of the Nile River. Having traveled extensively through Egypt, I am convinced that they were not built merely for pagan worship, but as sacred sites specially selected by spiritual initiates in order to expand their wisdom and understanding. Those on the path of enlightenment in ancient Egypt would begin at the upper part of the Nile and journey from temple to temple until each of their seven chakras had been opened.

At the culmination of their pilgrimage, the final initiation would take place at the Great Pyramid of Giza. This ceremony, according to some, required the participants to physically dematerialize their bodies in order to pass through the solid granite plug blocking the entrance to the King's Chamber. (Read *Initiation* by Elizabeth Haich or *Initiation in the Great Pyramid* by Earlyne Chaney for profound insights regarding these sacred ceremonies.)

Many books, including *The Aquarian Gospel of Jesus the Christ* by Levi, record that Jesus was initiated in the Great Pyramid at Giza during His "missing years" prior to His ministry.

The sacred energy of both the temples and the Great Pyramid can be perceived even today. Those who tour the Nile River and visit the series of temples can directly experience this energy. It is possible to feel the energy of these sacred sites in the area of the body corresponding with the specific chakra that it was designed to open.

On the outskirts of Cairo, the Great Pyramid and the adjacent Sphinx are positioned in the center of one of the most intense power vortexes in the world! Following a sunrise meditation between the paws of the guardian Sphinx, Shirl and I, as part of a small group of traveling companions, were allowed to enter the Great Pyramid early one morning before it was open to the public.

During our allotted three hours, we recreated an ancient ceremony inside the King's Chamber. Each of us in turn laid in the open, stone sarcophagus, an ancient symbol of death and rebirth centered in the otherwise empty, rectangular chamber. The incredible spiritual intensity was beyond description! Some reported out-of-body experiences. Others met their higher selves or master teachers. No two experiences were identical and no one was unaffected.

Just before we left, someone suggested we form a circle around a five inch tall, oblique crystal which we had placed on the floor in the center of the room. Someone began to chant "Oooommmmmmmmm," the universal mantra. Joining hands, we each added our voice to this reverberating sound. We focused our attention on the crystalline energy collector, which had been set on the altar in each temple where we had previously celebrated a ritual.

Without warning the crystal began to *move!*

Almost imperceptibly at first, it rocked back and forth as if it had somehow been awakened by ancient magic. It slowly rose several inches off the floor, paused in midair and then dramatically slammed to the stone floor, landing on its side and breaking cleanly in half!

No one said a word; it was almost as if it had been expected!

As you might anticipate, many documented stories and legends revolve around this Great Pyramid at Giza. One concerns Piri Reis, a Turkish seafarer. Among his possessions was found a map which has been authentically dated to 1513 A.D. It shows the European and African continents, including a survey of Antarctica's coastline *under the ice cap!* Considering that most educated people at that time believed the world was flat and somehow balanced on the back of a giant tortoise, this map is extraordinary.

The Great Pyramid is located in the exact center of Piri Reis' map, indicating it was the central place of world power at that time. As one moves toward the perimeter of the drawing, one finds that the amount of distortion increases. It is almost as if it had been drawn from a photograph taken directly above the pyramid with a wide-angle lens, a possible explanation for the foreshortened proportions that appear toward the outer edges of the map! Since this map dates from the same era as Christopher Columbus's earliest explorations, how could such accurate knowledge be obtained without a physical, aerial survey?

Is it possible that such information was derived from extraterrestrials? Their early visitations could explain the origin of Egyptian legends about Isis, Osiris and Anubis. Such ancient visitors from the stars would have been considered gods. They also might have been the inspiration for numerous cave drawings scattered throughout the world and thought to be portrayals of spacecraft and aliens.

Many ancient documents, such as Sumerian texts from neighboring Mesopotamia, record the actions of "gods" whose origins were from the sky. These stories, dating back to 4000 B.C., have given these visitors the name "din.gir," translated as "the pure ones of the bright-pointed objects." Ancient Sumerian renderings display clear depictions of "rocket ships" along with humans saluting them. Since there are ever-increasing numbers of people who actively subscribe to the theory that our entire species originated from distant star systems, such as the Pleiades, Orion or Sirius, who is to say this is not a plausible explanation?

Those who believe in the existence of Atlantis generally acknowledge that the Atlantians chose Egypt and the pyramids as the repository of their knowledge prior to the destruction of their continent. Several popular books expound the theory that ancient records and spiritual truths are buried near the bases of the pyramids. The fact that not long ago a large boat was found in the sands alongside the Sphinx confirms this conjecture for many.

Unlike the peaceful energy of the Delphi area, the energy in Egypt is strongly male and powerfully speaks of truths long forgotten.

In England, many people seek the ancient energies surrounding the stone monoliths scattered throughout the countryside, Stonehenge and Avebury being among the most famous. To conclude that these were constructed as astronomical observatories may not be the entire truth.

At Stonehenge, due to the ever-increasing crowds of people, visitors are no longer permitted to enter the ring of stones. But just before closing, after the tourist buses have departed, it is possible to recapture the essence of the special spiritual energy that remains from centuries past.

Although the main axis of Stonehenge is directly aligned with the rising sun on midsummer's day, it is difficult to imagine that star-charting was its sole purpose. The discovery of spiritual relics dating back more than 5,000 years makes clear the fact that this was a spiritual site long before the present ring of stones was erected. Just as most of

Europe's large cathedrals were built on sacred energy sites, it is commonly accepted that the builders who constructed Stonehenge's stone circle selected a traditional ceremonial location previously used by earlier celebrants.

In the small country village of Avebury, the road snakes through a separate, large circle of freestanding stones that are hardly noticeable at first as they have been placed some distance apart from each other. A second ring appears inside the first, then a third inner circle, which has a diameter of about a 100-feet. The circles are less defined and not as tall as the ones at Stonehenge, and there are a half-dozen houses interspersed throughout the area. The 180 stones forming these three circles, some weighing up to 60 tons, are thought to have been placed in their present location for ceremonial purposes well over 4,000 years ago. At dawn, in the absence of people or tour guides, walking among these stones is a peaceful, spiritual experience.

Within a mile or two of Avebury is Silbury Hill, the largest man-made ceremonial mound in Europe. This is the same area in England where the unexplained crop circles mysteriously and regularly appear in the nearby wheat fields.

Glastonbury Abbey and the nearby Tor are two more of a dozen or so spiritual energy vortexes in the same area of the British Isles. The Abbey is built on a location that Christ is said to have visited and blessed. It is also the documented site of the first Christian church in the British Isles, which, according to legend, once housed the Holy Grail, and it is where, in 1191, King Arthur was said to have been buried. His search for the legendary Holy Grail was, in effect, a search for spiritual awareness. Prior to the construction of the church, the Celts, the Saxons and the Druids considered this piece of ground a sacred energy place.

Many energy sites can be located by understanding the concept of geomancy and lay lines. Geomancy is the study of the patterns of natural energies inherent in the earth, and lay lines are the courses these energies follow. Many believe there are flows of energy circulating all over the earth, like veins in the human body, which can be observed in aerial photographs. The alignment of large geographical objects, such as groves of trees, large boulders, hills, lakes and mountain ridges, suggests the pattern these lines follow.

Nowhere are these energy lines more visible than in the British countryside. The dozens of stone circles that existed here at one time were all built along sections of these natural earth veins. The locations of these sacred English sites are sporadic yet geometric as the energy lines spread out linearly and join the sites together in a string. Masculine in nature, the energy speaks to advanced knowledge and ego. In these areas of energy, one can truly feel the power of the Middle Ages and the glory of what once was the vast and powerful British Empire.

To enhance one's sensitivity at a natural energy spot, a person should approach it by spiraling into its center, walking in a counterclockwise direction because spiritual energy flows in a counterclockwise direction. When leaving, spiral out in a clockwise direction, creating the grounding energy which will close down spiritual sensitivity and promote adjustment to the exterior world.

Ever notice that to lift a screw out of a piece of wood, we turn it in a counterclockwise direction? Similarly, to lift our awareness, we walk in a counterclockwise direction. To set a screw in place, we turn it clockwise. To return our consciousness to the physical plane and ground, we move clockwise.

The Haleakala crater on the island of Maui in Hawaii is home to the playful yet powerful energy of the Kahunas. The crater is a sacred energy spot of the ancient island natives. Present-day visitors are advised to pay respect to the island spirits, or, custom has it, tragedy may follow.

Witnessing the sunrise from the top rim of the crater is truly an unforgettable experience. One leaves the warmth of the Polynesian beach and ascends 10,000 feet in a few hours to a very cold and stark environment. As the sun appears over what seems like the edge of the world, one can truly feel the magic of creation.

And to witness the sunrise from *within* the crater is to be at one *with* creation!

To descend into the crater is to visit a moonscape. The trail from the top crisscrosses a quiet and still world, so sacred that no one ventures off the path for fear of leaving footprints in the volcanic dust. When in search of one's self, it is a place of retreat; the energy is extremely serious, powerful and feminine.

Many overnight campers within the crater have related stories of nighttime visions and psychic experiences. This site amplifies the specific thoughts and moods of the intruder; therefore, one should always arrive with pure intentions and have a true desire for spiritual learning. Anyone who carries off the volcanic rock may incur the wrath of the unseen inhabitants. On the other hand, those with respectful, clear intentions will be nurtured by feminine energy forces.

Sedona, Arizona, is located in the midst of the peaceful, red-rock land of the high desert. Native American tribal legends speak of "The People," or "The Ancient Ones," whose roots stem from the Grandmother Spirit of the world that still remains in the Sedona area. The Nizhoni, Anasazi, Hopi, Navajo, Apache and the Yavapai all claim to be descendants of this ancient culture.

In Sedona, the vortexes of both male (yang) and female (yin) energy are so well-known that they appear on tourist maps distributed in the visitor centers. Guides take visitors to vortexes, which number from four to nine, depending on whom you believe. The energy of these vortexes is vibrant; it awakens the male and female inner power of those entering a vortex vicinity. It is believed by some that this area contains remnants of energy from Lemuria, the peaceful continent that sank into the Pacific Ocean during the time Atlantis self-destructed.

Male or yang energy can be found at the Bell Rock and Airport vortexes in Sedona. They enhance masculine energy—ego clarity, self-empowerment, physical strength, commitment and many aspects of personal power.

At Cathedral Rock and Schnebly Canyon, female or yin energy inspires inner peace, spiritual awareness, sensitivity and the many and various facets of self-love. One may immerse oneself in the energy of Boynton Canyon to experience the healing combination of both the yin and yang energies. Walking through Oak Creek Canyon, touching the trees and stones while allowing the soothing sounds of the creek to flow through consciousness and carry away spent emotional debris, will be equally beneficial.

To experience Sedona is to let go, while, at the same time, opening to the harmonic frequency of true, multidimensional beingness.

Mt. Shasta in California and Machu Picchu in Peru are two examples of pure feminine spiritual energy on our planet. Pilgrimages are made to both places by people intent on bathing in spiritual intensity.

At Mt. Shasta, many on the spiritual path seek higher spiritual thought channeled by illuminated souls, such as St. Germaine. Those seeking this Christian counsel approach the beautiful, peaceful mountain with full reverence.

Others claim to contact beings from distant galaxies and/or other dimensions by way of telepathic communication, meditation or guided visualizations. The channeled information seems to vary depending on whom you ask, but the common theme always seems to be consciousness-raising.

A large society of people residing alongside the mountain even supports the notion that a community of non-physical light beings, who have survived the destruction of the continent of Lemuria, dwells *in* the mountain and uses it as a spaceport. UFO sightings are common and cloud formations around the top of the mountain often take on distinctive, spaceship forms.

Machu Picchu, the rediscovered "lost" city resting 10,000 feet high in the Peruvian Andes, has a wonderful, mysterious feminine energy. It was said to have been the spiritual fortress of the Incas, hidden even from the conquering Spaniards. Legend says it was a crystalline healing city in the days of Atlantis.

Some think that Machu Picchu is still an active port-of-call for intergalactic travelers. During mankind's early stages of development, these space or dimension travelers must have moved freely between Atlantis, Egypt and Machu Picchu. How else can one account for the giant leaps of knowledge these widely separated cultures experienced cyclically throughout the ages and the periodic, sudden and dramatic progress in human evolution between long periods of stagnation?

For confirmation, just ask Shirley MacLaine... in *any* of her incarnations!

And there are many other energy spots, such as the Aesculapian Dream Temple in Turkey, the monasteries of Tibet or the famous healing waters in Lourdes, France.

How can you experience them? Go find the ones that resonate in you.

Or just sit on a mountain top and experience the serenity. Walk into a natural circle of trees and touch the focus of nature's harmony in the center. Sit alongside the ocean and feel the power of the waves and, ultimately, of the universe itself. Each experience will increase the vigor of your journey of self-discovery along your individual path.

When you find your special energy spot, ask your spirit guides to minister their counsel to your soul. Experience increased self-awareness and allow your personal energy to intensify and merge with the power of the universal energy.

Look for the way home... for the path leads inward!

In the classic story *The Wizard of Oz*, remember how Dorothy suddenly found herself in a strange and unfamiliar land? If you recall, she was lost and was looking for the way home. She sought the help of the powerful and unseen wizard who lived far away in the Emerald City. After a series of wonderful adventures, she discovered that the wizard did *not* have the power to give her what she was looking for!

She had the power all along!

It was accessible through the ruby-red slippers she was given at the very *beginning* of her journey! Let's look at the symbols. Journey: her learning experience. Red: the color of the survival chakra. Slipper: her source of grounding and basic power!

Most classic stories endure and are universally accepted because they carry fundamental truths that we recognize—on a deep, inner level if not consciously.

Do *you* see the truth here?

Where was Dorothy's power to create what she wanted? She always had it, but if she hadn't had to search for it, she would have missed the adventure!

How did the slippers work? She clicked her heels three times, repeated the phrase, "There's no place like home,"... and *believed!*

Find your power spot in order to focus your power!

And then look for the way home... for the path leads inward!

CHAPTER 27

Feng Shui

As previously stated, *everything is energy.* As we interact with energy in its various forms, shapes and sizes, we develop perceptions and judgments and ultimately categorize most of our experiences as either positive or negative. It is, of course, human nature to view enjoyable occurrences as desirable and therefore good or positive. In a like manner, we conclude that difficult or disagreeable experiences are bad or negative, and we go to great lengths to avoid or minimize them.

Consider an alternative viewpoint: Everything which is, is good. We are told that everything is created by God, everything is God in physical form. If everything is God, the reasoning goes, everything is *good* because it was created for some higher purpose. But since we often do not understand this higher purpose, we often *perceive* individual objects, people or experiences as good or bad.

Perceive is the key word here. I imagine most of us are

aware by now that *what* we perceive as reality is altered by the manner in which we view it.

You might recall the story about the optimist and the pessimist, who are placed in a room full of horse manure. The pessimist is distressed for obvious reasons, while the optimist joyfully begins digging because he knows there has to be a horse in there somewhere! The point is that *what* we view as a positive or negative event is merely our perception of it.

Also, *where* we are affects our perception of an event. If we are at a location where energy vibrates at a rate compatible with our physical body, we generally have a more positive experience. No doubt you have perceived this environmental energy, perhaps without being consciously aware of it. For example, recall a time when you entered a new place and immediately sensed it as peaceful or pleasant. Conversely, recall an instance when you quickly departed or avoided a physical locale because, for no logical reason, it felt uncomfortable or threatening!

We, therefore, often attempt to change or alter the environment in order to perceive our experiences as being more positive. Many early cultures had specialists who worked with and altered the natural energy forces of our planet. These people were known by various names, such as witches, wizards, shamans, alchemists, priests, medicine men, elders and so on. (Some people today believe they currently exist in our society and are called politicians.)

The ancient Chinese have a word for the natural earth energy that leads to the creation of harmonious living and well-being; in fact, they have two words for it: "feng shui." Feng shui literally translates to "wind and water" and is held to be the Chinese art of placement, balance and enhancement of the environment.

Though records of feng shui can be documented to

the Fourth Century B.C., its concepts and practice most likely began centuries, if not millennia, earlier. As Chinese farmers first settled along the Wei and Yellow River Valleys, their human survival literally depended upon being in concert and harmony with the unpredictable forces of nature. They learned that to go against nature's balance would ultimately cause hardships, and so they took great care to avoid injuring the earth and the earth spirit, or in their terms, the flesh of the earthly dragon who exhaled a life-enhancing energy they called "ch'i."

Ch'i translates to "cosmic breath" or "energy," which is ascribed to all living things, including the atmosphere and the earth. It is this atmosphere and earth ch'i that feng shui experts seek to alter. They believe that since human life on this planet is tightly interwoven with the workings of nature and the universe, the proper channeling and enhancing of environmental ch'i will have a direct effect on human ch'i. Being in the flow of this energy can increase our individual happiness, wealth and vitality and dramatically improve our destiny.

Even in this modern era, many traditional Orientals hire a feng shui energy specialist to determine the proper location and setting of a new building in order to assure its harmony with nature and the happiness of its inhabitants.

According to the modern interpreters of the art of feng shui, several factors affect the resultant energy of a setting or dwelling and all those who encounter it. As an example, a house situated on a gentle slope is affected by ch'i that is much more smooth and even than the ch'i of a house on the top of a hill. The smooth ch'i brings greater peace and harmony. Houses located on rolling terrain are preferred to those constructed on flat, treeless land for the same reason.

The design of the approach to a structure also affects ch'i. Gently curved streets are best suited for carrying smooth ch'i, whereas straight roads convey ch'i too quickly and could cause disruptions. Structures at the end of a street are the least desirable as they are in the line of fire of the road's ch'i. The ancient Chinese would probably equate an automobile's headlights approaching along a straight-away with the glowing eyes of an oncoming tiger!

Walkways or driveways connect a building to the road's ch'i. A smooth, meandering and relatively level approach is best because it filters out bad ch'i. A semicircular drive-way is also desirable as long as the direction of its exit is consistent with the heaviest flow of traffic onto the con-necting street. Wide steps rising to the front door are said to conduct more desirable ch'i than narrow, descending steps.

The good news is that there are cures and methods that can negate undesirable ch'i. A fork-like driveway in front of the main entry door suggests that father and son may quarrel, thus causing the house to be in discord, but it is possible to eliminate the problem by painting red dotted lines or by laying bricks like dashes across the driveway or path. If a driveway narrows where it meets the street, the ch'i may invite dwindling career opportunities or decrease wealth-production. To cure the problem, one can install a lamppost at the narrowest point and spotlight it at the door or at the top of the roof. Or, better yet, one can widen the path.

And we haven't even begun to discuss the inner layout of homes and each room's proximity to the front door, or even the direction the bed faces...

Intrigued with this idea, Shirl and I invited a local feng shui practitioner to visit our home to determine what changes, if any, would create and maintain good energy in our environment.

When she arrived, our consultant first noted the natural terrain and other influencing structures in our neighborhood. She appraised the orientation of our house in relation to local, natural power spots, environmental landmarks and compass points. She then carefully considered our home's shape and style and the position of the main entry.

As she approached our front door, she paused several long moments, writing in the small spiral notebook she was to fill on her visit. Noting that one room is positioned forward of the front door, she asked about its function.

"It's our office," replied my wife in a voice that revealed her anxiety.

"Good," she said, smiling, "you want your financial center to extend beyond your entry door."

Shirl and I exchanged relieved looks because there was no other logical place for our office, and I was *not* about to undertake a major alteration to please the feng shui lady!

She slowly opened the front door and immediately stared at the wall that divided our entryway from the living room.

"Oh, oh," she frowned, "we could have a problem here."

Gesturing descriptively in the air with her arms, she explained that the six-foot-high wall partially blocked ch'i entering our house and could lower our expectations in life or lead to a struggle of some sort.

The contented smiles quickly dropped from our faces. She had barely entered our house and we were already one for two, batting .500. Major points had been deducted from our beginning score.

Reacting to the concerned expression on my wife's face and immediately sensing my resistance to even *considering* removal of the partial wall and the roof's structural supports, she smiled reassuringly. If we installed a mirror at the entryway to allow energy to penetrate the wall and hung bamboo flutes and feathers at key locations, she explained, we would have everything shipshape energy-wise.

During the next several hours she offered suggestions and minor corrections for each room, all the while jotting comments in her ever-present notebook.

As she wandered into the room we had converted into a playroom for our grandkids (the same bedroom where Shirl and I had encountered the ghost of her father shortly after he died), she stopped dead in her tracks!

"Ohhhhh... unsettled energy," she muttered.

Holding up her hand as if to stop further questioning, she walked the room's perimeter. When she was satisfied that she had an adequate understanding of the situation, she turned to Shirl and asked if any unexplained events had occurred here.

"How much time do you have?" Shirl asked, straight-faced. Then she briefly related the interactions with the ghosts of her dad and of Dick, her girlfriend's husband.

I told of several other unexplained occurrences over the years in this back section of the house and of my initial spooky reaction when I first explored it years ago. "The energy has never been threatening," I finished, "and we finally neutralized it after several crystal cleansings. I guess we have just learned to live with it, and it really doesn't bother us anymore."

"Some of our family and friends are nervous when they stay overnight," Shirl added, "but since we redecorated this area of the house, the ghost seems more comfortable and the lights don't blink nearly as much anymore."

Showing little reaction to our statements, our visitor commented that she needed something and briskly exited. We heard her open and then close her car door, but she did not reenter the house. Instead, she wandered, apparently aimlessly, around our front yard and then the back, all the while holding two black, L-shaped rods with the longest part extending in front of her, as if she were divining for water.

About 20 minutes later, she called for us to join her along the side of the house.

"I want to show you both something," she said in a low and serious tone. "Watch the ends of the rods."

She backed up a few steps and then slowly walked forward. As she did, the ends of the rods parted! She backed up and advanced again, repeating this movement three or four times. Each time the rods separated in the same manner and at the same location.

"Energy vortex," she stated matter-of-factly. "Could be a window where negative energy enters your house!"

Now, imagine how *you* would feel if someone discovered a negative highway from the astral plane leading directly to a bedroom in your house where previous ghostly encounters had taken place!

Palms perspiring, aware of the funny taste that always seems to deposit itself in my mouth in moments of stress, my mind replayed scenes from the 1980s movie *Poltergeist*. In this film, a family unknowingly constructs their house over an old graveyard, and the spirits who are disturbed begin to haunt the structure and its inhabitants. The credits of the film state that it is based on a true story!

"O.K., well at least we found it," the feng shui woman sighed in her soft-spoken way as she began to walk back toward the house.

"Wait a minute!" my wife and I shouted in unison. "What do we do now?" I asked, following the exclamation with the obvious question.

She did not respond. Instead, she offered me the rods. "Tell me what you think."

I held the rods as she had moments before, attempting

for the first time this ancient art of divination. Grounding myself by taking several deep breaths, I slowly walked forward with my gaze fixed on the ends of these two black metal rods.

With total amazement, I watched them separate *precisely* where they had for her!

I ran back to where I had started and repeated the exercise. This time the rods seemed to spring apart with a greater force, as two opposite magnetic poles once did in my high school physics class during a demonstration.

With a nod of her head, as if having just proved her point, our visitor again started back toward her car. "Don't worry. I have something that will take care of the problem."

"Have a hammer?" she inquired politely, returning with several small objects in her hand.

Without speaking a word, she went to the rear bedroom, paused a moment, then nailed a dime-sized, cheerio-shaped, purple oval to the baseboard just below the window where Shirl and I always thought our visiting apparitions entered. To depart, they always seemed to travel from this room straight down the hall and through the exterior door in the last bedroom.

The feng shui woman, gazing at what we indicated was the exit point, asked if the door had always been there. We explained that we had installed it several years ago as an emergency escape in case of fire.

"Any ghostly activity since you installed the door?" she asked, a barely detectable look of smugness on her face.

Shirl and I looked at each other, suddenly realizing that all of the major experiences had occurred *prior* to the installation of the door.

"I'm not surprised," she responded firmly. "The addition of the door allowed the apparitions to quickly flow through the house. Although the door is physically closed, it serves as an exit, and they haven't felt trapped as before. You shouldn't have anymore problems."

As she was about to leave, I told her that a confined passageway in another part of our home also made us uneasy from time to time.

"I know," she said as she walked out the front door. "I discovered the second vortex and installed another button to detour uninvited energy from entering your house."

Do I believe in this stuff?

You bet!

Can you do something about unsettled energy in your house?

Of course! Several suggestions...

First, purchase a book on feng shui and implement some of the suggestions. By merely installing a crystal, a plant, a mirror or a light in specific locations, you may immediately begin to sense subtle changes in the moods of those with whom you live.

By planting a tree or setting a small object, such as a birdhouse, birdbath, light, bamboo pole or other recommended object at specific locations around the perimeter of your dwelling, you may alter its exterior energy dimensions and easily introduce positive changes in the quality of your life.

There are other methods to cleanse or decrease negative vibes in the environment, too. For example, place a favorite quartz crystal in the center of your house and, with the assistance of others, imagine pure, white light emanating from its center and circling the participants. Collectively expand this spiritual energy throughout your dwelling, pushing unwanted energy out to be dissipated in the universe. Or create your own ceremony, anything from a spiritual house blessing of the kind performed routinely by Hawaiian native shamans to a simple gathering of friends for a house warming.

And if none of that works, know that you can always call on Freddy the Pig!

CHAPTER 28

Back to the Waterfall

It might be an appropriate time to pose what some feel is the ultimate question! It is a query that philosophers have pondered for centuries. The question is: *Why are we here?* What is the point of existence and our role in it... just what exactly is this gig all about anyway?

Descartes, as some of you might remember from your high school or college philosophy courses, asked whether or not we exist. This 17th century philosopher's well-known and often quoted conclusion was "I think, therefore I am."

On the face of it, Descartes' conclusion seems valid; it is an answer that is hard to refute! I'm here, or my consciousness is here or *something* is here, providing me with the experience of experiencing myself.

But *why*? *Why* are we here? *Why* does the universe exist? *Why* does existence exist and what is the ultimate purpose of it?

I remember asking my mother this question when I was

a child. After all, weren't mothers always supposed to know everything? (This was, of course, before I became a teenager and knew all the answers myself... all of which preceded my becoming an adult, venturing out into the real world and unexpectedly discovering that I didn't know as much as I had previously thought.)

"Why are we here? Why does the universe exist?"

My mother's answer: "Because!"

Now that's a great answer, and I accepted it when Mom's answers ruled supreme. But, as I grew older, I felt the need to know more!

If you were to ask mountain climbers what motivates them to climb the mountain, their answer would probably be, "Because it is there." This response might be applicable to the question at hand, but somehow it seemed to me that there had to be more to it than that, something more complicated, deeper!

I believe that I have always been seeking to resolve this question whether I consciously knew it or not. In one sense or another we all have. We attempt to sort out the clues and get a handle on the system and our small role in it.

Then, one day, a piece of the puzzle fell into place... at least a piece of *my* puzzle:

We have the answer! We've *always* had the answer.

It suddenly became apparent to me that life provides answers to *all* the questions. What we all seem to struggle with is learning what the *questions* are! Life seems similar in many respects to the television game show "Jeopardy," where the answer is provided and the job is to figure out the *question!*

The answers we are looking for already exist, and through the process of searching, we create the means of finding them!

Said once again, our individual consciousness is a portion of the larger experience (God) and *everything* occurring

in our reality has a purpose, including the process of looking for the answers.

And there is no one to look to for the answers... but
ourselves.

Christ said to go *within* to find the truth. The Eastern
religions teach that we can seek our answers through *in-
ward-looking* meditation. The answers, according to most
religious thought, *lie within.*

This hasn't always been the prevailing point of view,
however. As explained in Charles Van Doren's book, *A History of Knowledge*, St. Augustine wrote as early as the fifth
century about the existence of the "inner City of God." This
City, he explained, was clearly *separate* from the city of man.
St. Augustine's explanation regarding man's separation
from the Creator God, although challenged from time to
time, was generally accepted by religious scholars for nearly
1,000 years.

Later, in the Middle Ages, came a supporting notion
referring to what was called a "great chain of being." The
universe consisted of an ordered series of beings, beginning with the smallest living things and progressing to man
at the top of the chain, who was *separated* from a distant
and sometimes dispassionate Creator by an impenetrable
barrier.

Few in the past 1,500 years dissented from these basic
viewpoints. When the Italian theologian Thomas Aquinas
attempted to convince influential philosophers that man's
soul or spirit is at the juncture of the "two cities," which
were not as separate as commonly believed, he received
relatively little attention.

Then came the scientific and industrial revolution,
when precious little space was given to Aquinas or any other

radical and ordinary people were led to fully believe in the total separation of man and his Creator.

Only recently has modern thinking put a new spin on the old concepts. Arthur Lovejoy, in his classic book *The Great Chain of Being*, suggests that limited views and the "perennial philosophy" are changing. Now "men and women can grow and develop (or evolve) all the way up the hierarchy to spirit itself," Lovejoy states. They can realize and assume their identity as it relates with the Godhead. The separation between God and man that was assumed through most of modern history does not need to exist.

So, returning to my point, what better method of finding the *answers* to our questions than by using our psychic tools to go *within*. Remember, a psychic view of our past lives can provide insights enabling us to complete karma more quickly. Psychic communication with our higher guidance can allow us to maximize our spiritual growth more easily. Psychic manifestation can get us what we want more directly.

Once understood and used properly, our psychic perceptions can and will serve us. Why were they made available if they were not intended to be used?

Considering the above, the question "why are we here?" might now be answered, "We are here to *experience ourselves*, to learn pertinent lessons, to grow and to evolve!" In each incarnation we can retain the progress made in each moment, each day and each life, and we can build upon it lifetime after lifetime after lifetime...

And if you don't relate to *that* answer you might want to consider my mom's answer, "Because... "

It is important to consider both time and location when pondering life's great issues. Choose a time that feels right. Also, choose a space where the surrounding energy is likely to be safe, pure and supportive.

Why do you think prayerful people go to church and gurus retreat to the mountain top to talk to God or seek the truth? They seek a secure place with a minimum of distraction and illusion.

As previously discussed, such safe locations are called *power s*pots and are most easily found in nature—in the center of a natural circle of trees or rocks, near a waterfall, at the edge of the ocean or on ceremonial or sacred ground. You will feel drawn to *your* own power spot. This place will increase sensations of your own power, love and well-being.

One of my power spots is at the top of a 50-foot-high waterfall!

As related at the beginning of my story, Shirl and I were visiting friends in a remote area of Maui, Hawaii, who one morning took us to a magical location known only to a handful of local residents.

We rode in their four-wheeler along an isolated dirt road and then continued on foot along a seldom used path through beautiful tropical foliage and across several streams. Suddenly we came upon the magnificent, magical waterfall they had promised; it was like a picture on a travel brochure.

Wasting no time, our friends stripped to their bathing suits and plunged into the cold, clear pool at the base of the falls. They swam the length of this pond and disappeared through the pounding waterfall.

Shirl and I followed, emerging through the falling sheet of water into a well-hidden grotto, serene and peaceful, complete with tropical ferns and lush flora.

I recalled a story Ron, my host, had often told about a

family member who, on a dare, jumped from the top of a waterfall. I asked Ron if this was *the* waterfall.

"Funny you should ask," Ron responded with a smile that suggested maybe I shouldn't have. He disappeared back into the water and swam toward the rainbow curtain of mist, diving beneath the line of the descending falls. I followed. I did not have to be psychic to know where we were headed.

Ron lifted himself from the pool onto a rock, then onto another. In close pursuit, I stayed directly behind him, following in his footsteps. It seemed as if both of us were scurrying up the side of the pond's enclosing walls to get to the top before either of us changed his mind.

At the summit we carefully traversed the rim of the mini-canyon walls that led to the brink where the stream dropped to the pond below. Standing beside Ron at the extreme reach of a rock outcropping overlooking the water, I cautiously peeked over the edge.

"If I jump, will you follow?" Ron asked in a teasing voice that implied a dare.

"If *you* don't, I know I *won't*," I responded, choosing my words carefully to avoid a commitment.

Motionless at the extreme edge of the overlook, Ron reminded me of the Mexican cliff divers I'd seen in Acapulco, Mexico. Then, after carefully making minute adjustments with his toes, Ron jumped, leaving me both surprised... and *next!*

After incredibly long moments beneath the water, he shot to the surface, gave a Tarzan-like shout and swam to where Shirl and Barbara, Ron's wife, were observing the scene. Reaching for his towel, Ron looked up at me and smiled, his expression powerful, a confirmation of his accomplishment.

I looked down at the three small figures now standing together, keenly aware of their anticipation and concern.

Shifting my attention to the surface of the water below, I affirmed that the measurable distance of 50 feet was *much* different when looking *down* than when looking *up* from the ground.

My logical mind began to systematically list the many reasons why I should not follow Ron, yet I found myself inching forward. It was as if some outside force were drawing me. At the edge of the ledge where the water fell to the world below, I felt as if I were a passive observer, unable to deviate from some predestined script.

I knew that I was about to defy reason... *and logic.* Yet, to my own astonishment, I sensed only peace and calm. Present were neither heart-pounding sensations of fear that I always encounter when I confront heights, nor stark terror coursing up from the survival chakra. (Although I was in the construction business, I never got used to looking down from the edge on any of my unfinished structures.)

Then I heard it... an inner voice... from the very center of my being.

I knew it was *not* the verbalization of any of my guides, whose voices I had identified years before. This utterance was different. It came from within; it was as if it originated from unknown depths of the inner *ME.* I was assured that the next step was O.K., that *I* was O.K., that *everything* was O.K.. Along with this inner comfort, I felt an increased sense of personal power, a power I had never known existed. I knew without a moment's doubt that this was a significant moment in my life. I trusted absolutely. I'd been assured that it was safe to jump if *I* chose to do so.

Then, to my total amazement, I lifted my right foot, pushed off with my left... and was airborne!

What happened next is difficult to explain in words.

Time suddenly structured itself differently. Life's clock switched to slow motion. Peering down, I imagined that it would be minutes, maybe hours or even days before I broke the plane of the water's surface below me.

I also noted that I was both *experiencing* and *observing* my reality simultaneously.

Glancing over my shoulder at the descending sheet of water falling directly beside me, I suddenly recalled a childhood memory in overwhelming detail. In this vivid recollection, I was in grammar school and was observing myself in class. I listened to my teacher describe how Galileo dropped two differently weighted objects from the Leaning Tower of Pisa to determine if they would fall at identical rates of speed. I saw my classroom-self question and doubt the reported conclusion that they landed simultaneously in spite of their weight difference.

Well, I am here to report that the theory is correct! In my midair flight, astonished, I observed that the lightweight water droplets and my somewhat overweight body were plummeting at the *same* rate. The myriad, individual drops fell at the same speed as I did, appearing as if they were glittering jewels frozen in space. It was nothing like the usual blur made by falling liquid.

As I lowered my eyes again, my mind understood that my journey to the pool below had just begun. I would be measuring my progress in tiny inches and long moments.

To report that I received total clarification and resolution of many personal issues during this seemingly eternal free-fall would be an understatement. There was a *lifetime* of realizations in those few seconds of clock-measurable time!

My *perception* of time had been dramatically altered and expanded, confirming Einstein's theory that time is indeed relative to the observer.

MY jump experience and the experience of those OBSERVING the jump were two widely differing realities... and yet they were BOTH correct!

By the "time" my feet hit the water, I knew that I had been empowered by way of a major-league experience!

The icy water and the depth of my plunge were of little concern. I had passed through a gateway into a new level of experience—in spite of my limited belief systems and convictions. In that incredibly long/short moment, I had integrated a complete personal transformation, successfully discarding old tapes which, though confining, had served as the core of my being. And, on top of that, I had survived!

My leap into the air was a symbolic disconnection from old ways, freeing me to soar to a new level! As I reflect back, I now realize that it was the *second* step of a three-step, life-altering procedure.

In the first step, years before, I *discovered* my inherent psychic ability. Once I recognized the gift I had been offered, I awakened to a sense of greater purpose and freedom and a new way of being.

In the second step, I crossed the threshold of intention by leaping off the cliff into the unknown and *accepted* the freedom and the power which accompanied it. I was soon directed to the third and final step, *commitment.*

Discovery... acceptance... commitment!

Remember the three steps to manifestation. You must first know what you want—discovery. You must then know that you have it—acceptance. And finally, you must let go, let it happen—commitment!

Only after all three steps have been fulfilled will this law of manifestation operate.

It took me decades of living in a state of limited awareness before I made the *discovery* of what I really wanted...

the freedom to express my true self. By uncovering my psychic awareness, I learned that I was both the cause and effect of my reality. I had to experience limits and confinement before I could break those bonds to discover and accept the freedom to be me!

By jumping off the waterfall, I took the second step, the step of *acceptance*. I proved to myself that I possessed the personal power necessary to confront and defeat fear, which is the largest single limitation to the manifestation process.

The third step—*commitment,* the letting go and trusting part of the equation—was about to occur.

I have since revisited my magical power spot with Ron and Barbara. We walked the same trail and forged the same streams. Upon arriving, we again dove eagerly into the pond and swam through the thunder of the falling water. Before leaving, all four of us climbed to the top of the waterfall, taking turns at peering over the edge to the pond below. Without many words spoken, each of us knew that there would be no jumpers that day. My experience before was so extraordinary that it seemed appropriate to respect it for what it was.

Plus the fact… our wives said, *"No!"*

CHAPTER 29

The Last Chapter: The Bottom Line

To allow the law of manifestation to operate, you must *trust* that you will find that which you are seeking and *commit* to obtaining it. At the same time, you must discard all the reasons for not finding what is yours, what has been available and waiting for you all along. This *trust*-with-*commitment* is the last element required for manifestation.

I was about to have a dramatic encounter with this third principle!

Shortly after returning from Hawaii, I was forced to reexamine the future direction of my construction business in light of an approaching recession, an over-built construction market and a changing financial environment. I felt stressed and handcuffed by my analytical mind. My 2 + 2 = 4 building contractor persona, trained to function exclusively within the theater of logic, was incapable of resolving my burdensome dilemma. Finally, in desperation, I turned to my intuitive/psychic self for direction, even though I'd only completely trusted it before for emotional and spiritual direction. I withdrew to the sanctuary of my back yard to enlist the full moon and her companion stars in a standing meditation.

Years before, Gerri, my psychic mentor, had shared stories about Albert Einstein, her famous mathematician uncle, who had perfected four separate and distinct methods of meditation to accomplish different things. He would meditate lying down when he wished to be healed, sitting when he desired divine inspiration, walking when he needed to hear his own thoughts more clearly, and standing when he was problem solving.

If standing was good enough for Albert, I figured it was certainly good enough for me, and I proceeded to clear my mind and ask my higher self for guidance.

Afterwards, although my conscious mind was certain that no direct answers had been provided, I had a feeling that a solution to my quandary was at hand. Peering about for some sort of sign, I noticed that I had mindlessly drawn a straight line about three feet long in the dirt beneath my feet. Knowing that there are few "coincidences" in life, I began to focus on what this line was trying to convey. Placing my feet behind it, as if it were a starting line in a foot race, I realized that this mark could be a boundary. Perhaps I was being coaxed to commit to one side or the other, as if some sort of choice were being offered.

Suddenly, the old Walt Disney movie version of Davy Crockett at the Alamo projected on the screen of my consciousness. In the scene which unfolded before me, I saw Davy dramatically imploring those who wished to volunteer for the fight with the numerically superior army of Santa Ana to step over the line that he had drawn on the ground before him. He was asking them to make a *commitment!*

As I stood with my toes to my line, it became apparent that I, too, had just been asked to make a personal commitment!

But, a commitment to what? My psychic work? My business? My life? If this was some sort of test, I was unclear as to the question, let alone the range of possible answers!

It was during the process of asking aloud for clarification that a likely answer came: "ALL of the above!" If I were to cross over the line, I would have to *commit* to freedom— freedom from anxiety, freedom from all that blocked me from my true calling, freedom to be *me!* I did have a choice here. I could actually distance myself from the ever-increasing pressures of the family business, which were beginning to tell on my nearly 50-year-old body. To be free, however— and this was the punch line—I would have to *close* the successful business that had begun a generation before.

Immediately my defensive, left brain neurons fired up! I *couldn't even consider* this radical course of action. What about my employees? How about my son, who had recently joined the firm... and my father, who was still semi-active? What would I do? How would I survive? What would other people think?

It was as if I were observing a tennis match between two players volleying, each employing diametrically opposed styles of play...

I peered down again to the line I had scratched in the earth. *No way* was I going to cross it and take a senseless, irreversible step. *No way* was I going to walk away from the only profession I knew. In an irrational and emotional moment of weakness and self-doubt, I could not casually discard all that I had spent so many years building up.

As I walked back toward the house, I wondered how I could have even *contemplated* such a move.

The following evening, while watering my back yard, I happened upon the line I had drawn in the dirt. Some unexplainable inner urging made me lay the hose aside and cautiously approach it. Confident that my analytical logic was in place, I felt safe.

However, for the briefest of moments, I speculated on what it would be like *if* things were different and I *could* close my business. I almost felt the joy the freedom would bring, but it was a make-believe, "fairy tale" situation. I, of course, lived in the "real world." Abandoning my business was totally out of the question.

The third night, I again found myself standing in the footprints left from the previous two evenings. Again it was clear that I could not cross the line, yet this time I contemplated what it would be like when I retired and shed the responsibilities and stress that came with the territory. Naturally I couldn't do it now, but for the first time I knew that someday—in the far distant future—I would take that fateful step.

The fourth night, after returning home from a pressure-filled workday, I walked outside to confront the line. I toed my mark, closed my eyes and waited, as if this were a normal end-of-the-day procedure, like eating dinner or brushing my teeth.

Nothing!

Nothing happened. Nothing but *calm, stillness* and an *overwhelming sense of peacefulness!* I kept my eyes safely hidden behind my eyelids, reluctant to return my consciousness to the external reality I knew was out there, waiting for me. When I finally opened my eyes, I glanced down to the ground and felt an unexpected jolt.

The line was NOT THERE!

My heart raced. Mysteriously, some playful quirk of the universe had removed or erased the line. Had I been projected into the future? Perhaps the yellow brick road to the Emerald City of Oz passed through my back yard.

Then, quite by chance, I glanced over my shoulder. I was shocked at my discovery. *The line had somehow relocated itself BEHIND me!*

I swear I had not moved! In some magical fashion, my line of confrontation and commitment had relocated itself. The only plausible explanation was that the earth had suddenly shifted... or maybe one of my guides or guardian angels had carried me over to the other side, because there was *no way I would have moved over the line myself!*

That night, unable to find a rational explanation for what had occurred, I went to bed totally bewildered. Equally mysterious were the overwhelming sensations of *peace* and *completion* which permeated my entire body. All I could be certain of was that some type of "energy shift" had taken place.

During my commute to work the next morning I knew, without question now, that I would announce to my staff my decision to *close down the business!* My sense of incredible relief proved conclusively that I was being led to the proper action. While my logic-self was concerned about my economic future, my inner higher guidance was providing overwhelming assurance.

Even though I was training my son to assume the profession of my father's father and take up a family business that had served our ancestral line very well, I knew it was not his primary calling... nor mine. That business was *not* what made my heart sing, and I was not to question what was taking place, but simply get out of the way of the momentum that was by now well under way.

The bottom line was that I believed in and submitted

to my higher knowing. I had both *trusted* my spirit guides and *committed* to follow what they knew would be in my best interest.

Now that I had acted on my inner voice, I was faced with a dilemma. How was I to survive financially? I surely did not wish to work for someone else in the construction industry.

"Trust the process" was the repetitive, inner response.

About two weeks later, I received an unexpected telephone call from a tenant who leased part of a small shopping complex in which I had an ownership interest.

"Would you consider releasing us from our lease commitment?" asked the voice on the other end of the line. "Our business is being merged with another company, and we would like to consolidate both operations in their nearby location."

"Yes, of course," I responded firmly. My decision was an easy one because they were paying far less than the current market rate on a long-term lease.

Astoundingly, within the month I leased the same space for nearly double the amount my previous tenant had paid.

"Trust," said the small echo from the deep recesses of my being.

It must be clearly understood that it is risky and difficult to defy both tradition and logic. Tradition is an unwritten law which orders us to follow long established customs. Logic is the primary process we have been taught to rely on when making critical decisions.

In my situation, *tradition* implied that I was to train the family's fourth-generation contractor. *Logic* asserted that only the foolhardy would abandon an established, successful business institution.

Intuition said otherwise!

For the record, within a year of closing my business, economic recession, overbuilt conditions, bank and lending institution failures and increasing competition forced the majority of union construction businesses into hard times. By listening to my higher self and defying tradition and logic, I avoided major personal and financial crises.

I acknowledged guidance, and I took action. So, since *you* trusted whatever guided you to read this book, *trust* that you can begin the first day of the rest of *your* life by putting into practice the tools you have discovered here. Now that you know the process, manifest what you want and need. Experience!

I remember one of the first books I read on the subject of duality, the concept which says that anything in existence can be understood best by experiencing its opposite. For example, to comprehend light, one needs to experience the presence of darkness (the absence of light); health cannot really be appreciated until one has experienced sickness; and so on. The author described the concept in relentless detail, his many points illustrating the supposition with nothing left out. Finally, after an extensive summary, the final sentence of the book began with the words, "You have been told all you need to know about duality except for just *one* thing,... "

When I turned to the last page, the sentence finished *"duality does NOT exist!"*

Nearly 200 pages were devoted to explaining this theory from every conceivable angle, yet the author concluded in his last four words, duality *does not exist!*

What did he mean?

We each have to experience our individual separation and isolation (duality) before we can comprehend that, in truth, we are a portion of the larger ONE. As the book claimed, duality does not exist. It is only an illusion in this physical-existence-schoolhouse on planet Earth. The only thing that exists is the ONE.

Take a difference of opinion between two parties as an example. It is not that one person is correct and the other in error. Both interpret their own truth from their individual viewpoints. Both experience their separate truths (plural)! Even though they seem to be diametrically opposed, *both are correct.*

TRUTH is ONE (singular)! There is no duality!

The point is that we each have to learn all there is about life's duality and separation before we can be ONE with the Source. Alchemists knew this principle way back when. A central tenet of alchemical philosophy is that what we experience as a major problem—serious illness or business failure or even the death of a loved one—is the beginning of the "Great Work: spiritual transformation."

"Decay is the beginning of all birth... the midwife of very great things," and this is "the deepest mystery and miracle that He (God) has revealed to mortal man," wrote Paracelsus, a renowned philosopher, physician and alchemist of the sixth century. (From *Paracelsus: Selected Writings*, edited by Jolande Jacobi.)

In psychological terms, this means that completion (ONE) is only achieved when the many sides of the issue are experienced (duality).

Alchemists worked with this principle when they transformed lead into gold. Notice that they did not start with another *precious* metal; they began with lead, the most common and ugly metal available. The work of this spiritual transformation begins the same way, with the *prima materia,* the basic matter.

Your author is stating with equal conviction that the universe is *not* the model they taught you in school. The *good* news is that the text-book-described universe is just an illusion. The *better* news is that you can alter your universe by changing your reality... by tapping into the metaphysical tools which have been provided for your use, many of which have been presented through the pages of this book.

... And the BEST NEWS is that there is NO BAD NEWS!

And with that said, know that when *YOU* change *YOUR* reality and create *YOUR* own universe to *YOUR* specifications, you can be assured that *YOUR* story also will end with...
... AND THEY ALL LIVED HAPPILY EVER AFTER!

The beginning...

About the author

Chuck Coburn, a native Californian, graduated with a B.S. in business from San Jose State University in 1962. Then he worked with a construction firm for eight years before forming Coburn Construction in 1970.

Chuck was 35 and "cruising through life with the statistically average family." His company was lucrative and prestigious. He thought he had it all. Then one Sunday evening in 1975, to Chuck's total astonishment, he discovered he was psychic.

From that day forward, as his psychic occurrences continued, Chuck's life underwent a 180 degree change. Letting go of his commitment to the left brain logical thinking process, he allowed his newly discovered abilities to lead him through the many soul searching adventures, studies and experiences about which he writes.

Since 1978, Chuck has served as a professional psychic channeler and counselor. He regularly conducts workshops and seminars, and he lectures to high schools, colleges, organizations and private groups. He has appeared as a guest on numerous radio and television shows and is a host on "Personal Pathways," a Northern California cable TV program.

Chuck teaches his clients how to develop their own psychic gifts and to access their higher consciousness. His own higher guidance prompted him to write this book to illustrate that opening to one's psychic awareness is something we all can do.

About the cover artist

Kendra Barron uses the process of painting to explore the meaning of life. She has taught art in public schools and pursued a career as a painter and printmaker. Kendra has designed sets for California Theatre Arts, Walnut Creek, and produced and directed the video, "Taoism: Releasing the Power of Creativity" (1989).

Her current project is creating the 64 Doors of Life, a series of large paintings that apply the ancient *I Ching* wisdom. Once completed, plans are to exhibit her doors throughout the world.

SEED CENTER

Enlightening classics

Initiation
Elisabeth Haich

Lazy Man's Guide to Enlightenment
Thaddeus Golas

Contact

Seed Center
PO Box 1700
Redway, CA 95560
707-923-2524